THE
RADICAL
TRADITION

THE
RADICAL
TRADITION

R·H·TAWNEY

Twelve Essays on
Politics, Education and Literature

Edited by RITA HINDEN

With an appreciation by HUGH GAITSKELL

PANTHEON BOOKS

A DIVISION OF RANDOM HOUSE

New York

In 1960, when Tawney attained his Eightieth Birthday, a large gathering of his distinguished friends was held in the House of Commons, and a brochure on his life and work was published. A number of his friends felt that it would be fitting if the occasion were also marked by the publication of a number of his articles and essays which were no longer available to the public. Tawney was dubious whether a book could be made from this scattered material but he responded to the suggestion by bringing together the material. His literary executors—Sir Richard Rees and Mr Michael Vyvyan—felt it would be a grave loss if these papers could not reach a public interested in the work of this distinguished scholar and thinker.

Accordingly, Dr Rita Hinden was invited to edit the material for the purpose of this book. She was a friend of Tawney and shared his outlook on social and political questions; she is herself an experienced editor and author. She kindly undertook to prepare this book. Tawney's literary executors and I are grateful to her for the care and competence she has shown in this matter. We also acknowledge our thanks to the publishers for the facilities of publication which they provided.

A. CREECH JONES

EDITOR'S PREFACE

These twelve papers have been chosen from a pile of writings which Tawney had himself gathered together as possibly being suitable for republication after his death. One or two were in manuscript form, with no record of their having previously appeared in print, but most were newspaper articles, pamphlets published by different organizations—as wide apart as the Labour Party and the National Book League—or chapters which he had contributed to books of essays by various writers. Their dates of writing stretch over forty years—*An Experiment in Democratic Education* was written in 1914, and *The WEA and Adult Education* (the same subject!) in 1953.

But in spite of the variety in form, date, origin and length of this random selection of papers, they are all unmistakably 'Tawney'. In the first place, they deal with some of the subjects which were his special concern—social history, not least the history of British radicalism; education, particularly the imperative need for opening wide the doors of secondary and further education to all who wished to enter them; politics, especially the politics of social democracy as opposed to capitalism on the one hand and any form of totalitarianism on the other; industry, with the emphasis on according their rightful status to the workers within it.

In the second place, these essays provide shining examples of what Hugh Gaitskell described, in the postscript, as Tawney's 'special quality'—the combining of 'learning with passion'. The range of Tawney's scholarship was vast, but even those who knew him well might be taken aback by the scope revealed in the beautiful concluding essay on 'Social History and Literature'. And from swimming in these heady waters, he could turn quite naturally to the statistics concerning conditions in the coal-mines before 1914 (omitted from the paper on the 'Nationalization of the Coal Industry' as being irrelevant today). Yet this learning is shot through with passion—the passion for *equality* for all human beings, and the passion against the gross, materialist values of the *acquisitive society*. It was not chance that these italicized words are the titles of his two most famous books.

The last thing that Tawney could ever have been thought was a cynic. He was a confident optimist and an incorrigible enthusiast. In this third respect, too, the author has left his indelible imprint on the essays that follow. In 'The Conditions of Economic Liberty', written during the first world war, Tawney was quite convinced that we would emerge from the war into a far better world. In 'Social Democracy in Britain', written shortly after the second world war, when the Labour Government was in its prime, he cannot contain his enthusiasm for the new order being born in Britain. He was enthusiastic about the benefits of adult education and excited about the advantages of nationalization. He always insisted, of course, that nationalization was a means, not an end; its results depended on what men made of it. But he was optimistic about the results, and so he never faltered in his advocacy of the means.

This mention of 'means and ends' brings me to the reason why so many of us in the British Labour movement reverenced Tawney. Gaitskell has described him as '*the* Democratic Socialist par excellence'. I would go further and describe him as 'the Democratic Socialist *philosopher* par excellence'. He clarified for us, as no one else did, the distinction between the ends for which we were striving, the society in which the universal values of equality, freedom and fellowship found expression, and the institutional means, changing according to circumstance, by which such a society might be approached. There was no room for intellectual dogmatism in this approach; but there was also no compromise with the enemies of freedom for the sake of 'efficiency', 'productivity' or any material advantage, and certainly no mercy for the upholders of privilege. There have been many strains of thought in British socialism, many lapses from the purity of Tawney's creed, but in the final analysis, what he upheld represented our truest and deepest aspirations. The reader will find almost every facet of his beliefs scattered within the covers of this book.

One final, editorial word. Most of the essays have been abridged, sometimes quite considerably. Tawney had himself left notes indicating that radical cuts would often be required. In order not to interrupt the flow of his argument I have usually not shown where the cuts have been made, nor have I retained all his detailed footnotes. I have also followed Tawney's wishes in omitting factual and statistical material which has become out-of-date. The important thing is the *argument*, most of which is as true and fresh today as at the time it was written.

RITA HINDEN

Thanks for permission to reprint are due to the Athlone Press, the *Political Quarterly*, the *Observer*, the National Book League, *Socialist Commentary*, and to Bishop William Scarlett of Maine, US, who edited *The Christian Demand for Social Justice*.

CONTENTS

PART I

THREE RADICALS

I

WILLIAM LOVETT[1]

The Life and Struggles of William Lovett,[2] which is now reprinted from the first edition of 1876, is more than the mere autobiography which its title might suggest. Lovett was a Cornishman, born in 1800 at Newlyn, who migrated to London in 1821. From about 1825 onwards he was actively engaged in public work, and from 1836 to 1839 he was the spokesman of the political labour movement which started with the formation of the London Working Men's Association, and which developed into Chartism. Place, whom he knew intimately, described him as a 'man of melancholy temperament soured with the perplexities of the world', but 'possessed of great courage and persevering in his conduct', and remarked, 'his is a spirit misplaced'. Though without either the cool adroitness of Place, or the gifts of the mob-orator which made and ruined O'Connor, he was enough of a personality to be the leader of working-class politics in London. He was evidently one of those who are born to be given office by any organization with which they are connected.

Lovett's career—thrown out of work by the competition of a new trade, excluded at first by the union from what afterwards became his profession because he had not served an apprenticeship, craftsman, coffee-house keeper, agitator, prisoner, journalist and schoolmaster—is an epitome of the social confusion in which the working classes were plunged during the passage of industry from the old order to the new. As a member

---

[1] This paper appeared as the Introduction to a new (1920) edition of Lovett's book.
[2] *The Life and Struggles of William Lovett*, in his Pursuit of Bread, Knowledge, and Freedom. With some Short Account of the Different Associations he belonged to and of the opinion he entertained. Vol. I. (London: G. Bell & Sons, 1920.) The quotations from Lovett are all taken from this book; those from Place from Graham Wallas, *Life of Francis Place*.

and afterwards president of the Cabinet-makers' Society, storekeeper to the first London Co-operative Trading Association, secretary of the British Association for Promoting Co-operative Knowledge, a member of the Grand National Consolidated Trades Union which blazed up for a few months in 1834, founder and secretary of the London Working Men's Association, secretary of the Chartist Convention of 1839, secretary of the National Association for Promoting the Political and Social Improvement of the People, and a delegate to Sturge's Complete Suffrage Conference in 1842, he saw from the inside almost every popular movement of the thirties and forties. He attended the London Mechanics Institute, where he heard Birkbeck, and possibly Hodgskin, lecture; was a colleague of Cleave, Hetherington and Watson in their agitation for a free Press; had his furniture sold because he refused to serve in the militia 'on the ground of not being represented in Parliament'; knew reformers and prophets of the old generation and the new, Cobbett, Hunt, Carlile, Cobden and Owen, whose principles he absorbed, while resenting his autocratic methods; denounced, to the annoyance of Place, who was working for unity, 'the Whig Reform Bill'; petitioned Parliament for temperance reform and the opening of museums on Sundays; reasoned with Melbourne as to the legality of public meetings in Lincoln's Inn Fields, while 'a posse of the new police were posted in the next room' to protect the minister against the deputation of desperadoes, and fought the battle of the trade unions when they were threatened with a revival of the Combination Acts in 1837. Above all he was the secretary of the London Working Men's Association, and drafted the document which was afterwards published as the People's Charter. He was careful to preserve the manifestos and addresses, many of them written by himself, in which the various organizations with which he was connected, in particular the London Working Men's Association, expounded their views to the working-class public of Great Britain, Ireland, Canada, the United States, Belgium and France.

Lovett had certain limitations both of experience and of character which make his account of the Chartist Movement, if taken by itself, liable to mislead the reader. His adult life was spent in London, and he was perhaps a little inclined to see the rest of England under the optical illusion which residence in London is apt to create. Birmingham was his *ultima Thule*, and, a fact which had disastrous effects on the leadership and fortunes of Chartism, he did not know or understand the north. Like most thoughtful workmen of the time he loathed the new industrialism—'children forced to compete with their parents, wives with their husbands, and the whole society morally and physically degraded to support the aristocracies of wealth and title'. But he was not himself of it. A skilled craftsman and a member of an ancient and exclusive trade union, he had no first-hand knowledge of industrial England, with its turbulent population of miners and cotton operatives, swept together, without traditions or organization, in towns which were little better than mining camps. To that as yet undisciplined force, which, led by O'Connor, snatched the Chartist movement after 1839 out of the hands of London and carried it forward on a wave of misery and violence to its ignominious collapse, Lovett, by temperament a student and a teacher, make little appeal. Like Sir Charles Napier, the most discerning and most chivalrous of enemies, who as general in charge of the northern command averted a collision compared with which Peterloo would have been child's play, he regarded the 'physical force men' as the worst enemies of his cause. But, unlike Napier, he does not seem to have understood the tempest of despair and indignation which responded to the denunciations of Bull and Stephen and Benbow, which prompted the midnight drillings on the moors, raised barricades in Staffordshire, and at Ashton-under-Lyne burst into the cry 'O ye Tyrants, think you that your mills will stand?'

While Lovett's book contains only a fragmentary account of the later years of the Chartist movement, the picture which it gives of its genesis and earlier development is invaluable. During the creative period, when doctrine was being formulated and methods thought out, the London Working Men's Association was the centre of Chartism, and Lovett was the centre of the Association. From the first there was a double strand in Chartism. On the surface it was a continuation of the demand for the reform of Parliament as a step towards political democracy. Like the fathers of the movement fifty years before, the Chartists demanded manhood suffrage—Lovett himself

17

believed in adult-suffrage and annual parliaments: their additions were the four other points, equal electoral districts, vote by ballot, payment of members and abolition of a proper qualification. It was characteristically English that what afterwards became a semi-revolutionary movement on the part of the working-classes, of whom none had a vote and almost all appeared to most members of Parliament a band of ragged ruffians, should pour its grievances into the parliamentary mould. Unfortunately, it was hardly less characteristic that, of the powers of this world, hardly one had the wit to thank Heaven for the inveterate constitutionalism of his fellow-countrymen.

Though the Charter was political, Chartism was largely economic. It was, as Marx pointed out, the entry in politics, not merely of a new party, but of a new class. The English counterpart of the continental revolutions of 1848, it was at once the last movement which in this country drew its conceptions and phraseology from the inexhaustible armoury of the French Revolution, and the first English political attack upon the new social order born of the growth of capitalist industry. The declaration that 'all men are born equally free, and have certain natural and inalienable rights', marched hand in hand with the doctrine that 'Labour is the source of all wealth'. Capitalism upon a large scale and in a highly concentrated form was still sufficiently novel in the thirties to seem not only repugnant but unstable. It was the revolt against capitalism which made the magic of Chartism to thousands of men who were too wretched to be willing to subordinate the passion for economic change to the single issue of political reform. Behind it lay two generations of social misery and thirty years of economic discussion, which had percolated into the mind of the working classes partly through popular papers, such as the *Poor Man's Guardian* and the *Co-operative Magazine*, partly through the teaching of the early English socialists, Thompson, Hodgskin, Gray, and above all, Robert Owen. The essence of Chartism was, in fact, an attempt to make possible a social revolution by the overthrow of the political oligarchy.

These two objects were not incompatible. But in an age when the mass of the working classes were without either organization or political experience, they were not easily pursued together. The struggle between the conflicting interests of economic reform and political democracy, corresponding as it did to a difference in outlook between north and south, and to the rival policies of revolution and persuasion, ultimately broke up the movement. The achievement of Lovett and of the organization which he founded was to create an Independent Labour Party which aimed at both, but which put political democracy first.

The London Working Men's Association was established in June, 1836, as the result of two great disillusionments, the Reform Act of 1832 and the collapse of the syndicalist movement launched by Owen in 1834. The first had taught it to be independent of middle-class leaders. 'The masses, in their political organizations,' writes Lovett, 'were taught to look up to great men (or to men professing greatness) rather than to great principles. We wished, therefore, to establish a political school of self-instruction among them, in which they should accustom themselves to examine great social and political principles, and by their publicity and free discussion help to form a sound and healthful public opinion throughout the country.'

The failure of the Grand National Consolidated Trades Union had at once left an opening for a political movement, and emphasized the necessity of making the basic political reforms upon which the working classes agreed rather than social theories upon which they differed. Lovett himself, though in later life he repudiated the ambiguous name of Socialist, was in his youth a disciple of Owen, and believed 'that the gradual accumulation of capital by these means (i.e. Co-operation) would enable the working classes to form themselves into joint-stock associations of labour by which (with industry, skill and knowledge) they might ultimately have the trade, manufactures and commerce of the country in their own hands'. But, on the principle of first things first, he was resolute that the London Working Men's Association should concentrate its energy upon securing political reform. It was not to be 'led away by promises of repealing the detested Poor Law, or any of the other infamous laws which Whig and Tory have united to enact, and to laud their excellence, unless the promise be accompanied by the pledge of universal suffrage, and all the other great essentials of self-government'.

The London Working Men's Association was, even at its zenith, an extremely small body. The total number of members admitted between June, 1836, and 1839, was only 279. Its objects were to agitate for parliamentary reform, for the freedom of the Press, and for the creation of a national system of education, and to collect and publish information upon social and industrial questions. Its method was education and propaganda. At a later stage in its career the character and policy of the movement started by the association were transformed by the very success of its earlier efforts. From the early months of 1837 onwards it employed 'missionaries', who, by the end of the year, had founded over one hundred daughter associations in different parts of the country. The publication of the People's Charter in June, 1837, enormously increased its prestige and multiplied its adherents. Chartism was taken up by veteran agitators like Benbow, who could look back to the days of the Hampden Clubs and Peterloo, and politicians in search of a platform like Beaumont and O'Connor.

The agitations against factory slavery and the detested new Poor Law swelled the main movement and cast their own sombre colour upon it. But for the first three years of its existence the policy pursued by the London Working Men's Association had nothing in common with the orgy of mob oratory in which Chartism finally collapsed. Its appeal was to public opinion: its instrument argument and persuasion—'to publish their views and sentiments in such form and manner as shall best serve to create a moral, reflecting, yet energetic public opinion; so as eventually to lead to a gradual improvement in the condition of the working classes, without violence or commotion'.

Lovett's policy of working for gradual reform through the pressure of public opinion was, of course, no novelty. But it was in striking contrast both with Owen's apocalypse of a new moral world, which was to descend upon mankind 'like a thief in the night', and with the whirlwind campaign of sterile denunciation and fantastic promises, which fed the vanity of O'Connor. Neither economic circumstances nor the attitude of the ruling classes made Lovett's course easy. At a time when whole districts lived on the edge of starvation, and when the Government seized every opportunity to crush peaceful attempts at organization, the restraint and foresight needed to concentrate on slowly won political changes, which, in turn, could only very slowly bring social amelioration, were qualities not easily to be maintained. Revolt seemed a more direct route than persuasion.

Lovett had no illusions as to the character and policy of the Government. He had been dogged by its spies, had seen the savage onslaught upon trade unions from Dorsetshire to Glasgow, and knew that it at once hated and feared any symptom of independent political activity, even of independent thought, among the working classes. In language reminiscent of the Whig doctrine that a breach of the original contract absolves men from the duties of obedience, he argued that 'When an attempt is made to destroy representative rights, the only existing bond of allegiance, the only power through which laws can be justly enforced, is broken, and the time has arrived when society is resolved into its original elements'. Tireless in preaching moderation and patience, he was prepared to consider in the last resort what came to be called 'ulterior measures'.

But he regarded violence as the last weapon of defence, not as part of his political offensive. For the hare-brained rhetoric which made violence certain of occurrence and futile when it occurred, for the policy of coquetting with revolution while appealing, at the same time, to the spirit of the constitution, and of coming, to quote a characteristic specimen of O'Connor's oratory, 'morally into collision' with the Government, he had all the contempt of the genuine craftsman for the antics of the charlatan. Down to the end he believed that one principal cause of the defeat of Chartism was that the advocates of physical force had driven all waverers on to the side of reaction. 'Whatever is gained in England by force, by force must be sustained; but whatever springs from knowledge and justice will sustain itself.' It was necessary to choose whether to appeal to goodwill and reason, or to organize an insurrection, the fate of which it did not need the military experience of Napier to foretell. He chose the former.

The methods of the London Working Men's Association were

determined by his choice. 'Such Associations,' wrote Place, 'can only succeed by long-continued, steady, patient, liberal conduct, accepting and using every kind of assistance which may at any time and in every way be available, making no absurd pretensions to anything, and especially not to superior wisdom and honesty, but acting with becoming modesty, and with indomitable perseverance.' During the first three years of its existence, the London Working Men's Association carried out Place's programme. Secrecy was to be eschewed. There was to be no talk of violence. Middle-class support, whenever possible, was to be enlisted. Such use as was possible was made of the small and not too reliable group of radical members of Parliament.

In the meantime the Association laboured to influence public opinion by a stream of reports, addresses and manifestos setting out the working class point of view as to contemporary political and social questions. The range of subjects covered by them is remarkable. They give a broad and generous interpretation to the political aspirations of labour, and are singularly free from the exclusive preoccupation with immediate economic issues of which popular movements are often accused. In addition to the agitation for the reform of the franchise, which was its main work, and the case for which it set out in the pamphlet, 'The Rotten House of Commons', it produced reports on the condition of the silk weavers of Spitalfields and on education. It issued a manifesto defining the attitude of the Chartists to the agitation for the repeal of the Corn Laws, in which, without imputing the motives afterwards ascribed by some Chartists to the manufacturing and commercial interests behind the free trade agitation, it combated the suggestion that an alteration of the tariff was more important than the enfranchisement of the working classes. In 1837, when the disorder accompanying a strike of cotton spinners in Glasgow led to the outrageous sentence of seven years transportation being passed on certain members of the union, and to the appointment by the Government of a Select Committee to inquire into the whole subject of trade unionism, the Association undertook much the same part as had been played by Place and Hume in 1824 and 1825. It appointed a Trade Combination Committee, arranged with societies to send witnesses, issued an 'Address to the working classes in reply to the attacks made on trade unions', and generally attempted, in 1837 a somewhat forlorn hope, to secure that the unions had fair play.

From the beginning the Association claimed the right of the working classes to be heard on international and colonial affairs. It addressed a manifesto to the working classes of Belgium on the occasion of the imprisonment of Jacob Katz, petitioned Parliament on behalf of Canada against the policy of coercion adopted by Russell, sent an address of sympathy to the Canadian people, and published manifestos to the working classes of Europe, to the Precursor Society of Ireland, and to the Irish people. The National Association of the United Kingdom, which after 1840 did the work formerly done by the London Working Men's Association, was almost equally prolific. It not only produced a number of manifestos on its special subject of Parliamentary Reform, but continued the international tradition of the older organization. It denounced the reception of the Czar, on the occasion of his visit to England in 1844, issued in the same year an 'address to the working classes of France on the subject of War', and in 1846, when feeling ran high on the question of the Oregon boundary, published 'an address to the working classes of America on the war spirit sought to be created between the two countries'. In 1848, when the Revolution in France had revived for a moment the golden dreams of 1789, it sent a congratulatory address to the French, urging them to prepare themselves 'intellectually and morally for the coming age of freedom, peace and brotherhood'.

These manifestos, the majority of which were by Lovett, contain in epitome the philosophy of Chartism. Their fundamental ideas are four.

(1) Social evils are the consequence of social institutions, and can be removed by altering them. The speculations of the nineteenth century upon the causes of economic misery had begun with the debate between Malthus and Godwin, and in one guise or another most subsequent thought marches under one or other of those rival banners. The argument that it is the natural tendency of population to press upon the means of subsistence had pacified uneasy consciences among the middle classes with the assurance that the evils of society were the work

of nature not of man, and after 1850, when economic fatalism had been reinforced by the triumphant gospel of evolution, the mind of labour for a time submitted to that creed.

From 1820 to 1850 the leaders of working class thought were in revolt against it. They drew their weapons from the forgotten armoury of pre-Marxian Socialism. Godwin, who explained to young men in 1793 the nature of the new force which was overthrowing thrones and castles in France, and whose 'Political Justice' was reprinted in 1843, at the height of the Chartist movement, and Owen, who had found Godwin a confirmation of his own doctrine of the all-importance of environment, had taught them that character is formed, not by man, but for man; that in a world where the external order was just and reason allowed full play he would progress swiftly towards perfection; and that there was no force within him, no original sin or intractable remnant of the tiger or ape to drag him down. At the end of the eighteenth century Paine and Spence had turned on the English system of land tenure criticism which Chartists used in the thirties and forties. A host of critics of capitalism had pointed the antithesis between increasing wealth and increasing poverty. Colquhoun, the first statistician of modern capitalism, and Ricardo, the Balaam of economic science, whose curious fate it was to supply the cornerstone to doctrines which he detested, by insisting that labour is the source of all wealth had given a new sting to the inevitable question 'Why, then, is the labourer poor?' Above all, Owen had supplied reformers with an ideal for which to work, the Co-operative Commonwealth.

Chartism absorbed these ideas and made them the basis of a political movement. If wealth is rightly distributed, there is sufficient for all. Poverty is not due to scarcity but to unjust social institutions. 'By many monstrous anomalies springing out of the constitution of society, the corruptions of government, and the defective education of mankind, we find the bulk of the nation toiling slaves from birth to death—thousands wanting food or subsisting on the scantiest pittance.' The land, 'which a bountiful Creator bestowed upon all his children', is 'engrossed and held in possession by comparatively few persons', who render no service in return for it, though in legal theory its tenure is conditional on the performance of public functions. Manufacturers and capitalists, 'by their exclusive monopoly of the combined powers of wood, iron, and steam . . . cause the destitution of thousands . . . and have an interest in forcing their labour down to the minimum reward'. As a result, the workers 'submit to incessant toil from birth to death, to give in tax and plunder out of every twelve hours' labour the proceeds of nine hours to support their idle and insolent oppressors. . . . The greatest blessings of mechanical art are converted into the greatest curses of social life.' The theory of surplus value, in all but name, is already in existence.

(2) From a social philosophy of this kind Syndicalism springs as readily as political agitation. But Syndicalism had been discredited by the failure of the Owenite movement of 1834, and its failure left the field clear for a renewal of the attack on Parliament. The cause of social evils is Government by a political oligarchy which has an interest in maintaining them. 'The people . . . now perceive that most of our oppressive laws and institutions, and the consequent ignorance and wretchedness to which we are exposed, can be traced to one common source—Exclusive Legislation, and they therefore have their minds fixed on the destruction of this great and pernicious monopoly, being satisfied that, while the power of law-making is confined to the few, the exclusive interest of the few will be secured at the expense of the many.' Nothing is to be hoped from existing parties, for Whigs and Tories are equally the enemies of the working classes. The House of Commons is not so much ignorant of social evils as indifferent to them. 'While our social evils and anomalies have repeatedly been brought before you, you—whose duty it was to provide a remedy—have looked carelessly on, or have been intent only on your own interests or pleasures. Your own Commissioners have reported to you that thousands of infant children are doomed to slavery and ignorance in the mines and factories while their wretched parents are wanting labour and needing bread.' The remedy is political democracy, 'a Parliament selected from the wise and good of every class, devising the most efficient means for advancing the happiness of all'.

The language of Chartism is sometimes reminiscent of Bentham's statement that the Government is a fraudulent trustee who uses 'the substance of the people as a fund out of which fortunes might . . . nay ought . . . to be made', that the king is 'corrupter-general', the aristocracy at once 'corrupted and corrupting', and that 'Corrupter-General and Co.' is, therefore, the proper title of the firm. But the difference in spirit between such a work as the Utilitarian James Mill's *Government* and democracy as conceived by Lovett is immense. To the former the State is not a band of brothers, but a mutual detective society; the principal advantage of popular government is that there are more detectives, and therefore, presumably, fewer thieves. To Lovett democracy is less an expedient than an ideal, the vision of liberty, fraternity, and equality which had intoxicated men's minds in the days before Liberalism was shorn of its splendours and its illusions. He is, in fact, a 'Social Democrat'. 'To justly distribute the blessings of plenty which the sons of industry have gathered, so as to bless without satiety all mankind—to expand by the blessing of education the divinely mental powers of man, which tyrants seek to mar and stultify—to make straight the crooked path of justice and to humanize the laws—to purify the world of all the crimes which want and lust of power have nurtured—is the end and aim of the democrat.'

The instrument by which popular government is to be established is Parliamentary Reform. Manhood suffrage is a natural right, for 'as Government is for the benefit of all, all have equal rights, according to their abilities, to fill any of its offices; and, as the laws are said to be for the benefit of all, all should have a voice in their enactment'. It is in accordance with the spirit of the constitution and has been proved to be beneficial by foreign experience. It is the only guarantee against misgovernment and the one remedy for economic oppression. The argument that the masses are too ignorant to vote comes with a bad grace from governments which are at pains to keep them in ignorance. Political wisdom comes from the exercise of political power. 'Political rights necessarily stimulate men to inquiry, give self-respect, lead them to know their duties as citizens, and, under a wise Government, would be made the best corrective of vicious and intemperate habits.'

(3) The condition of any genuine democracy is education: to work for the creation of a national system of education is the first duty of reformers. It is the one certain instrument of

emancipation. 'Imagine the honest, sober, reflecting portion of every town and village in the kingdom linked together as a band of brothers, honestly resolved to investigate all subjects connected with their interests, and to prepare their minds to combat with the errors and enemies of society . . . Think you a corrupt Government could perpetuate its exclusive and demoralizing influence amid a people thus united and instructed?' To withhold it is the most cruel of wrongs. 'Is it consistent with justice that the knowledge requisite to make a man acquainted with his rights and duties should be purposely withheld from him, and that then he should be upbraided and deprived of his rights on the plea of ignorance?' The governing classes have purposely made access to knowledge the privilege of the rich. 'Though the time has gone by for the selfish and bigoted possessors of wealth to confine the blessing of know-ledge wholly within their own narrow circle . . . yet still so much of the selfishness of caste is exhibited in their fetters on the Press, in their colleges of restriction and privilege, and in their dress and badge-proclaiming charity schools, as to convince us that they still consider education as their own prerogative, as a boon to be sparingly conferred upon the multitude, instead of a universal instrument for advancing the dignity of man and for gladdening his existence.' Education is 'not a charity, but a right, a right derivable from society itself . . . It is the duty of the Government to provide the means of educating the whole nation.'

When Lovett wrote these words, four years had elapsed since Parliament made the first grant of £20,000 towards elementary education. In the preceding thirty years two education bills had been introduced and rejected. It was not till 1836 that the duty on newspapers was reduced, and not till 1855 that it was abolished. Historians of education have described the gradual process of enlightenment by which the ground was prepared for the establishment of the rudiments of something like a national system of education in 1870. But they have done something less than justice to the popular movements which demanded access to knowledge at a time when plans for the education of the working classes were regarded by a consider-able section of opinion as not less absurd, and considerably more dangerous, than the proposal to educate animals. If public education in England still suffers from the defects of a system devised by one class for the discipline of another, it is partly because the efforts of working people themselves to promote it met in the past with frigid or indignant opposition.

When Lovett wrote of 'the hawks and owls of society seeking to perpetuate the state of mental darkness', and of 'the Utopians who failed to perceive that God had made one portion of mankind to rule and enjoy, and the other to toil for them and reverently obey them', he spoke from bitter experience. The first and greatest of working-class educationists, he himself was one of the Utopians. He had pursued knowledge with a passion which undermined his health, and which is not easily intelligible to those whose lives have been cast in more pleasant places. He was zealous to make it accessible to others. The background of his efforts was the doctrine and experiments of Owen. 'Any general character,' Owen had written, 'from the best to the worst, from the most ignorant to the most enlightened, may be given to any community, even to the world at large by the application of proper means; which means are to a large extent at the command and under the control of those who have influence in the affairs of men.' What means these were he had shown at New Lanark. Chartism, like Co-operation, absorbed eagerly this aspect of his teaching. The London Working Men's Association gave education a prominent place in its programme. One of its earliest manifestos was an impassioned appeal for the creation of a national system of education. Chartist schools and churches sprang up in different parts of the country. The pamphlet 'Chartism', which Lovett wrote in prison, was an educational tract rather than a political manifesto. The National Association for promoting the Political and Social Improvement of the People, which was founded in 1840, proposed to establish circulating libraries, to erect schools for children and normal schools for teachers, and to offer premiums for essays on educational subjects. One school, at least, was actually established in London, and was managed for some years by Lovett himself.

If the practice of these reformers was crude, their educational projects were more generous and enlightened than anything which has yet been brought into existence. Education was to be free, universal, secular, financed from public funds, and administered by 'school committees', elected by adult suffrage, and acting under a Committee of Public Instruction appointed by Parliament. Training Colleges were to be established, and none but certificated teachers were to be allowed to teach in the public schools. No sanction was given to the arbitrary and mischievous division between elementary and secondary education, which is the misfortune of a system organized on the basis of class. Elementary education was called by its right name—preparatory education—and was to be followed, as a matter of course, by the education of the adolescent. There were to be Infant Schools, held as far as possible in the open air, for children between three and six years of age, Preparatory Schools for children from six to nine, High Schools for children from nine to twelve, and Finishing Schools or Colleges for all over twelve. University education, like the earlier stages, was to be free. The schools were to be open in the evening for the further education of adults. Religious instruction was to be given out of the ordinary school hours. Of course, no Government could be expected to notice such fantasies. If any had, some dark chapters in social history might never have been written.

(4) The cause of democracy is international. The Governments of Europe take common action, when they can, to suppress all movements for reform. 'Though the despots of the world may quarrel for territory or plunder, they are cordially united to keep the people in subjection.' An agitation which threatens one is regarded as the enemy of all. 'The friends of freedom throughout the Continent have just cause to remember with feelings of execration the base conduct of the Government of England in secretly maintaining or openly opposing every attempt they have made to check the inroads of despotism or to advance the cause of democracy.' The people are helpless, for they are not informed as to foreign policy. The statesmen who attack democracy abroad are the very men who stifle it, when they can, at home. The tyranny from which the working classes suffer in England is the same as that which has ruined Ireland, which has produced an attack upon the liberties of the Canadian people, which used English soldiers and sailors to put down republican insurrections in Spain, and which on the Continent has led to the enslavement of Poland and Italy.

Lovett's indictment of the existing international system is

naturally couched in somewhat general terms, as any criticism of a system jealously guarded from popular observation must be. The claim that international policy should be judged by popular opinion marks more definitely, however, than any other point in the Chartist programme the emergence of a new force in public affairs. It was hardly possible to be connected with political agitation in the London of the thirties without coming into contact with unquiet refugees from the continental reaction. In 1844 Lovett took part in founding a society—'The Democratic Friends of all Nations'—composed of English radicals and exiles from France, Germany and Poland. In such an atmosphere internationalism came naturally to those engaged in popular movements. If the early English socialists anticipated the fundamental economic conceptions of Marx, it may be claimed as truly that the idea of the International, with its appeal 'Workers of all lands, unite', was present to the minds of some of the leaders of Chartism.

The London Working Men's Association was the first English organization to produce manifestos for foreign consumption. They strike a note which has found since then a thousand echoes. The common economic interests of the proletariate are more profound than its national divisions. 'We address you in that spirit of fraternity which becomes working-men in all the countries of the world . . . the subjugation and misery of our class can be traced to our ignorance and dissensions . . . the tyrants of the world are strong, because we, the working millions, are divided.' The combination of the governments must be met by a combination of the peoples. 'Fellow-producers of wealth! Seeing that our oppressors are thus united, why should not we, too, have our band of brotherhood and holy alliance? Seeing that they are powerful through your ignorance, why should not we unite to teach our brethren a knowledge of their rights and duties?' The 'aristocracy have waged' wars 'for the preservation of their order'. But 'the interests of our class are identified throughout the world', and consist, above all, in peace. The working classes of all lands 'by whose industry the munitions of war must be raised . . . who are mainly selected to be the tools and instruments of warfare . . . who must perform the bidding of some aristocratic minion, were it to be war against freedom abroad or to exterminate your brothers at home', must unite to maintain peace. When in 1844 there was tension between the French and English Governments, the National Association published an address to the French working classes urging a united protest against war, and proposing the establishment of 'a Conference of Nations, to be composed of three or more representatives, chosen by the people of their respective countries, to meet annually, for the purpose of settling all international disputes that may arise by arbitration, without having recourse to war'.

After 1842 the brains were out of Chartism. After the fiasco of 1848 it collapsed altogether as an organized movement. The worst period of economic misery was over. The edge of the industrial system was slightly blunted by the Factory Acts of 1847 and 1850, and the Public Health Act of 1848. In the triumphant outburst of commercial prosperity which began about 1850, both the idealism and the struggles of the heroic age were for a time almost forgotten. The energy of the working classes was diverted from political agitation into building up co-operation and trade unionism on a firm financial basis. Some of the reforms which the Chartists had demanded came at last, with the Reform Acts of 1867 and 1884, and the Ballot Act of 1872, though after the lapse of a generation and in an attenuated form. Lovett lived to see the Education Act of 1870 and to denounce its inadequacy.

His own verdict on the struggles of his youth was that the Chartists had been right, and that political independence was the only hope of the working classes. 'Most of the reforms that have taken place in my day have been won rather in despite of the wealthy and titled classes, than owe to them their origin, though they might at last have been made the unwilling instruments for carrying them into effect. So long, therefore, as those who are aiming at cheap and wise government help by vote or voice to place persons who have neither interest nor sympathy with them in the position of representatives or rulers, so long will they be putting obstacles in their own paths. The industrious classes, therefore, would do well . . . to resolve to do their work themselves.'

2

ROBERT OWEN[1]

It is primarily as an evangelist, expounding in the infancy of the Great Industry the principles of a social order sharply antithetic to that foreshadowed by it, that Robert Owen is today remembered. But the hero of the socialist legend found his way to fame by a path which few others trod. Successively shop-assistant; mill-manager for whose services Lancashire cotton firms competed; head, when under thirty, of a great manufacturing concern; pioneer of reforms later a household word; for a time a celebrity whom statesmen on both sides of the Atlantic heard with mingled incredulity and respect, Owen, for all his reputed Utopianism, was not a child in the ways of this world.

The luckless American ventures, which cost him his fortune, and his return from the United States to discover that, during his five years absence, his publications had made his name the symbol of popular discontents and aspirations, opened a new chapter. But his seminal ideas had taken shape in the days when, as an industrialist, he had beaten at their own competitive game the rivals who ridiculed as ruinous the methods employed by him, and had attacked, not as a victim, but as a conqueror, the anti-social egotism of the raw capitalism of his day. The works which added new chapters to his gospel, and did most to make the enlarged version known, belong to the latter part of the same phase of his life. Beginning in 1813 with the *New View of Society* and ending with the *Report to the County of Lanark* in 1821, they were the product of the years when, though already a public figure, he was still firmly anchored by his New Lanark roots.

A career so disjointed lends itself to caricature. It is easy, by fixing attention on the business magnate, or the promoter of the quarrelsome Elysium of New Harmony, or the Messiah of the

[1] A review article (unpublished?) on a biography of Robert Owen, presumably written in 1953.

New Moral World, to produce a portrait at once accurate and distorted. Mrs Cole's lively, well-proportioned, and not uncritical biography[1] avoids that snare. On some points, in particular the trade union upheaval of the early 1830s, it has fresh light to throw; but its value is less the additional information supplied by it than its success in enabling the not too obviously related aspects of Owen's multifarious activities to be seen by the reader as an intelligible whole. It consists in the skill with which the authoress portrays the struggles of a personality idealistic and practical, credulous and shrewd, dictatorial and at times absurd, but sustained amid all its vagaries by a pertinacity resembling that of Milton's Gryphon in the wilderness, first to cure the evils of the small community of which it took command, and then by successive campaigns on broader fronts to transform the social system which produced them. In the former task the reformer succeeded; in the latter he failed. But the principles of the master remained a power in quarters sceptical of his methods. The vision, perpetually discarded and perpetually revived, of a Co-operative Commonwealth owes more to Miss Martineau's 'gentle bore' who 'always meant something more rational than he actually expressed', than to any other individual before the days of William Morris.

Owen had left the village school of Newtown as a boy of ten. He may later have been influenced by the discussions of the Manchester Literary and Philosophical Society; but his humanitarian labours drew their dynamic, not from education and books, which, he characteristically remarked, 'the radical errors shared by all men make of little value', but from a secularist version of the Inner Light. Convinced early in life that he had discovered the secret of social regeneration, he was thereafter driven forward by a remorseless demon of benevolence, whom no successes could satisfy, and no failures arrest. The rationalist psychology shared by him with Bentham, who surprisingly liked him enough to put money—'his only successful investment'—into New Lanark, disposed Owen to accept, not Utilitarian economic theories, than which nothing could have been more repulsive to him, but a conception of the springs of conduct resembling, in its sweeping simplifications, the different analysis of the sage.

[1] *Robert Owen of New Lanark* by Margaret I. Cole, Batchworth Press, 1953.

His fundamental axiom, compared with which all other lights were dim, was that man is the creature of his environment, and that the habits, styles of existence and moral values of whole populations have been and can be transformed by changes in the conditions, natural, economic and social, in which their lives are spent. That conclusion, the premise of all his thought, if not the product of his experiences as an industrialist, was inevitably strengthened by them. The uncompromisingly dogmatic form, in which his statement of the omnipotence of environmental influences was cast, was a gift to critics; but the lesson laboured by him was that which governments, indifferent to the social revolution at work beneath their eyes, most required to be taught. Whatever theoretical qualifications his generalization might demand, two facts, he insisted, were beyond dispute. The first, as he told his fellow-capitalists, was that 'the pillar of the political greatness of the country is a manufacture which, as it is now carried on, is destructive of the health, morals, and social comforts of the mass of the people engaged in it'. The second was that the evils resulting from rapid urbanization and an unregulated factory system were not inevitable, but could, given the will, be averted or cured.

During his years at New Lanark Owen propagated his views less by precept than by practice. The benevolent despotism established by him is to be seen against the background of an age in which functions—today entrusted to public authorities—must be performed by the employer or not at all. His enlightened educational programme, with its insistence on the importance of the early years of life; its transference of emphasis from discipline to kindness; and its anti-scholastic bias, which gave observation, discussion, music, dancing and open-air activities a larger place in the curriculum than books, was, it seems, the child of his own brain; and the institutions based on it for long remained unique. The accompanying sanitary and housing reforms, the humanizing of management, the reduction of working hours, and the central store supplying wholesome provisions, were intended to do for the characters of those of mature years what the schools more hopefully did for the young. Together they made New Lanark a Mecca to which, in the course of ten years, some 20,000 pilgrims of different nations, from philanthropists, administrators and politicians to ambassadors, a Russian Archduke and the minister later immortalized by Shelley as his symbol of hypocrisy, resorted for edification and light.

In his combinations of business acumen with political *naïveté* Owen had a touch of the late Henry Ford. Rich, admired, and convinced by 1816 that the hour had come 'When I may call numbers to my aid', he was fired by the hope that his local improvements might be used as the basis of national reforms. His first modest step in that direction promised well, but ended in smoke. A factory bill drafted by him and introduced by a humane and intelligent cotton spinner, the elder Peel, was smothered by indifference in the House and the hostility of the textile interests outside it. The mutilated fragments which at last, three years later, emerged as an Act, were received by their parent with just contempt. His second effort at mass conversion was less specific in aim and more grandiose in scale.

There are words which lay a spell on the imagination of those using them. The term whose associations haunted Owen was Community. The capital fact of his day had been the technological triumphs which in the industry best known to him had, he alleged, increased twelvefold in a quarter of a century the output of wealth. Whether the result was a blessing or a curse depended upon the purpose to which the new powers were put. Owen's communal gospel was an eclectic and expanding faith; but in general it meant to him a society in which the co-operative efforts of partners would supersede the relation between employer and employed, and the ever-rising surplus of the age of plenty, which he believed to be in sight, would be used, not for individual self-advancement or display, but to 'create a rational, intelligent, wealthy, and superior population'. The emphasis on the deterioration of human quality as the capital sin of the economic system of his day, and on its improvement as the aim of all his schemes, was characteristic. It had inspired the cheerless title of the Institute for the Formation of Character which had crowned his New Lanark labours, and which he valued, not only for the activities carried on within its walls, but as the symbol and cement of a more social society. But how persuade his countrymen to accept his formula of salvation?

The post-war depression, with its attendant problems of

demobilization, unemployment, wages, Poor Law and agricultural distress, together with mental bankruptcy in high
places, gave him his chance. On some of these topics he had
already, in his *New View of Society*, made his opinions known.
Now, in the six years from 1816 to 1821, he expounded in
speeches and on paper his programme of agricultural communities, first, as in his *Report to the Committee for the Relief of the
Manufacturing Poor*, with the limited object of providing work
and maintenance for the unemployed, later as the starting-
point for more sweeping reforms. Owen was the last person to
impress the gatherings of London intellectuals and politicians
whom in 1816 and 1817 he harangued. Possibly publicity—'I
was the most popular individual in the civilized world'—had
gone to his head; but, apart from that pardonable fault, his
bland assurance of infallibility made him maladroit with critics,
and his apocalyptic propensities, though a trifle to what later
they became, were liable to set him soaring into mystical clouds
at moments when his only hope would have been both feet on
the ground.

Though, however, like Bentham's geometrical Panopticon,
and for much the same reason, Owen's 'Parallelograms of
Paupers', as Cobbett called them, were apt to cause hilarity, it
is a mistake to dismiss his projects as a mare's-nest. There was
not much to be said for setting unemployed craftsmen to work
on the land, but 'internal colonization' policies were later
pursued by more than one government. Owen's version of them
was taken seriously enough to be investigated by a committee
including such economic notabilities as Ricardo, Torrens and
Peel, with the Duke of Kent in the chair.

As subsequently expounded in the *Report to the County of
Lanark*, which he himself put high among his works, 'Mr
Owen's plan', as it was called, does not seem today of a kind
to excite either enthusiasm or despondency and alarm. It was
natural in the pre-railway age to think of social reconstruction
in terms of villages, not towns. Stripped of its frills and of the
hypothetical statistics dear to Owen's heart, his programme was
in essence a proposal for the establishment—whether by public
authorities such as counties and parishes, or by land-owners,
companies, and, a pregnant suggestion, associations of wage
earners, he did not greatly care—of a number of garden villages,

as today they might be called, combining agriculture with manufactures, and arranging production and distribution as seemed
to their members best. The virtues of the scheme which most
appealed to him were two. In the first place, the gross disparities of income which produced luxury at one end of the
scale, poverty and unemployment at the other, and waste at
both, would cease to exist. In the second, since education, a
healthy environment and cultural amenities would be shared
by all, it would be to the advantage of all to spend liberally
on them.

Disillusioned by indifference, and deprived by his partners,
who for good reasons and bad had lost patience with him, of
his control of New Lanark, Owen sought in the New World a
climate more congenial to panaceas than was offered by the
Old. In the meantime—such is the power of an idea—his
message was carrying all before it in quarters remote from those
to which, in his innocence, he had first looked for support.
Economic recovery and the liberalized Toryism of 1822 wound
up the post-war glacial age. Streams long dammed began again
to flow. Among them were the social aspirations which found
expression in the trade union revival encouraged by the Act of
1824; in the proliferation of societies which, whether strictly
co-operative or not, set co-operation and education in the fore-
front of their aims; in a renewal of the demand for drastic
factory legislation, and in the struggle of the political unions
for parliamentary reform. Thus, the atmosphere to which
Owen, when the New Harmony bubble burst, returned in
1829, was profoundly different from that of the England whose
dust, five years before, he had shaken off his feet. It was to
these popular movements that, rejected by the powers of this
world, he now appealed.

The relation between him and his working class disciples was
at once touching and odd. It was a blend of adoration on the
one side, sympathy on the other, and cross purposes, which did
not diminish, on both. In the eyes of thoughtful wage-earners
Owen was the prophet who had laid his finger on the mystery
of iniquity, and had preached a fraternal gospel by which the
capitalist demon could be brought to heel. Owenism, therefore,
was their religion, and its founder, who had suffered in fortune
and reputation for his faith, an idol. But their Messiah was an

exacting, and at times an imperious, chief. Modest in manner and intransigent in beliefs, he claimed with a mild, impersonal arrogance, regardless of such trifles as majority votes, the obedience due to the voice of inspired—or, as he would have termed it, rational-truth. His reputation, his personality and his prodigious propagandist powers brought thousands to his feet; but it does not seem to have occurred to him that the gates of the New Jerusalem need more than one key to unlock them, or that among those required, not only lofty principles, but knowledge, has a humble, but essential, place.

There were phases of the social ferment, therefore, from which, scenting fresh recruiting-grounds, he could not stand aloof, but on which his utterances were not, to speak with moderation, according to light. The trade union upheaval of the early 1830s is a case in point. Owen's scheme for a National Guild of Builders contained the germs of a suggestive, if then impracticable idea. It is evident, however, from his subsequent proposal for a Grand National Moral Union of the Useful and Productive Classes; from the part which he played in the short-lived Grand National Consolidated Trades Union of 1834; and from the zeal with which, at the height of embittered disputes, he reiterated invocations to brotherly love between masters and men, that, in dealing with matters of this order, he was off his beat. The truth is that his soliditarist preconceptions were too strong. They disabled him from understanding either the tensions from which trade unionism springs or the purposes which it serves.

Divided by his social pacifism from the militants of Organized Labour, he was separated from another and larger section of his adherents by a chasm equally profound. It was natural that the theorists of the pre-democratic era should visualize the social system of their hopes as bestowed from above, not as won by struggles from below. As far as the method of its establishment was concerned, Owen's Socialism, like Saint-Simon's very different version, was of that authoritarian genus. As first presented, in the days when he had access to the great, it was to be the gift of enlightened rulers, and then, when that devout imagination flickered out, was depicted, not as a work of political art, but as emerging from a mystical 'revolution of the human mind directed solely by truth, by charity, and by kindness'. On either assumption, the ordinary political processes, by which abuses are corrected and reforms introduced, were dismissed by him as irrelevant or worse. It is not surprising that a trade unionist and co-operator like William Lovett, secretary of the London Working Men's Association and later of the first Chartist Convention, should both have paid tribute to the influence on himself and his fellow-workers of Owen's social teaching and have repudiated with equal emphasis the political quietism of the master.

The course of public events deepened the rift. The struggle for the first Reform Act, disillusionment with its results, the collapse of the trade union offensive and hatred of the New Poor Law, combined with grievances of longer standing to cause radically-minded workers to see in the conquest of political power the first condition of all other reforms, and in Chartism the weapon to achieve it. Owen, on his side, moved the other way. His co-operative doctrines and phraseology left their mark in 1844 on the constitution of the Rochdale Pioneers Society, to which the modern Co-operative Movement is commonly traced, and long after his death historians of education and factory legislation were to do justice to his labours.

In his later years, however, his inexhaustible energies increasingly flowed in sectarian, and at times, transcendental, channels. It is easy to make merry with the ever-lengthening list of organizations, each with a title more resounding than the last, which he continued to produce with the effortless spontaneity of an oyster secreting pearls; with the failure of the community at Queenwood directed by him as Social Father of the Society of Rational Religionists; and with the harmonious dialogues which, in his spiritualist phase, he conducted with so agreeably mixed a company as the shades of Franklin, Shelley and the father of Queen Victoria. But, if a man has done in youth and middle age as much for his fellow-men as Owen did, only a curmudgeon will grudge him his ration of eccentricities after sixty-five. It is wiser to point with Mrs Cole to 'the rules of life which he sought to establish—kindliness, toleration, co-operation, respect for youth, the creation of a non-competitive environment'—and to agree with her that Owen has still some lessons to teach.

3

JOHN RUSKIN[1]

When Ruskin was writing for *Fraser's Magazine* the papers which afterwards appeared as 'Munera Pulveris', the editor stopped their publication before the series was completed, because the perversity of the author caused pain to the public; and long after Ruskin's books upon art had become classics his social and economic writings were dismissed as the eccentricities of a genius who had floundered into a sphere which he did not understand. But Ruskin was not a specialist in art criticism (if there is such a thing), who meddled with another specialism called Political Economy. He was not even a student with two interests, each of which he cultivated in turn, as a banker may be a historian or a man of science. He was a man whose sense of the moral unity of the world was so passionate that it impelled him to verify and expound it in one human activity after another, because, unless related to that central unity, all activities become meaningless and in time degenerate.

The essence of his whole thought about art and about society is that art and industry are not specialisms at all, but the expression in different forms of the faith which rules in men's minds, and which, therefore, finds its visible embodiment in their labours and their social organizations. As that faith is, so will their institutions and their activities be, and they cannot remove the defects which they deplore unless they are willing also to forego the success which they esteem, because both failure and success spring from the same false valuation.

'They read my words,' Ruskin once wrote, 'and say they are pretty, and go on in their way.' Many of the individual suggestions which shocked contemporaries as solecisms when he touched on them—the idea of a minimum wage, of equity in prices, of reasonable profits, of recognition of the status of

[1] Article appearing in the *Observer*, 19.2.1919.

worker—have since become commonplaces, and, in the controversies between Ruskin and the economists opinion today, even among economists, would probably be on the side of Ruskin. But though later generations have sometimes acted upon his stray hints, which he let fall in following his main argument, they have not submitted to that argument itself, because it has seemed too hard for them. And so, though they are more fertile in particular reforms, they are as far as ever from the synthesis to which he tried to lead them.

But it was this synthesis, and not the occasional practical illustration of it, which was his message, and which it is most necessary for us to absorb today. There are many people, indeed, who think that any attempt to formulate a synthesis, or to be guided by principles of any kind other than the convenience of the moment, is futile and, indeed, mischievous. Such people are at once much more common, and much more dangerous than those who resist all changes of any kind, as a quicksand is a more formidable obstacle than a stone wall. Men may genuinely sympathize with the demand for a radical change, but unless they will take the pains, not only to act but to reflect, they end by effecting nothing. For they deliver themselves bound to those who think they are practical because they take their philosophy so much for granted as to be unconscious of its implications, and, directly they try to act, that philosophy reasserts itself as an overruling force which presses their action more deeply into the old channels.

When they desire to place their economic life on a better foundation, they repeat like parrots the word 'productivity', because that is the word that rises in their minds, regardless of the fact that productivity is the foundation on which our economic life is based already, that increased productivity is the one characteristic achievement of the age before the war, and that it is precisely in the century which has seen the greatest increase in productivity since the fall of the Roman Empire that economic discontent has been most acute. When they are touched by social compunction they can think of nothing more original than the diminution of poverty, because poverty, being the opposite of the riches which they value most, seems to them the most terrible of human afflictions. They do not understand that poverty is a symptom and a consequence of social disorder, while the disorder itself is something at once more fundamental and more incorrigible, and that the quality in their social life which causes it to demoralize a few by excessive riches is also the quality which causes it to demoralize many by excessive poverty. So their well-intentioned schemes for social reorganization are abortive, because they endeavour to combine incompatibles, and, if they disturb everything, settle nothing. They are like a man who, when he finds that his shoddy boots wear badly, orders a pair two sizes larger instead of a pair of good leather, or who makes up for putting a bad sixpence in the plate one Sunday by putting in a bad shilling the next.

Yet all the time, Ruskin tells us, the principles upon which industry should be based are simple, however difficult it may be to apply them, and if they are overlooked it is not because they are obscure, but because they are elementary. They are simple, because industry is simple. 'The essential work of the political economist is to determine what are in reality useful or life-giving things, and by what degree or kind of labour they are attainable or distributable.' The purpose of industry is service, to supply men with the material means of a good life. Its method is association, the combination for one end of the different kinds of skill and energy which are necessary in order that the service may be rendered. The conditions of the right organization of any industry, therefore, are permanent, unchanging, and capable of being apprehended by the most elementary intelligence, provided it will read the nature of its fellowmen—in the large outlines of history, not in the bloodless abstractions of experts.

The first condition is that industry should be subordinated to the community in such a way as to offer the best service technically possible; that those who offer faithful service should be honourably paid, and that those who offer no service should not be paid at all, because industry is a social function, and it is the essence of a function that it should find the meaning in the satisfaction not of itself, but of the end which it serves. The second is that its internal arrangements should be settled not merely by considerations of economic expediency or convenience, but by principles which are recognized as just. The application of those principles should be the care of those engaged in it, acting, Ruskin sometimes suggests, through guilds, which will regulate the method of production and the quality of the product, because the condition of a healthy social life is order which springs from co-operation and freedom, combined with responsibility. 'The merchant or manufacturer's function is to provide for the nation. It is no more his function to get profit for himself out of that provision than it is a clergyman's function to get his stipend.' 'Government and co-operation are in all things the law of life; anarchy and competition the law of death.' These principles ought to determine both the relation of any industry as a whole to the community as a whole, and the relation of the different parties within an industry to each other. In so far as a nation observes the first, it will be faithfully served; in so far as it observes the second, it will secure justice for those who serve it.

'It is believed,' Ruskin wrote, 'that the first object of the merchant or manufacturer in all his dealings must be to get as much for himself and leave as little to his customers as possible.' It is indeed. And because men believe this, they believe also that they can discover short cuts by which they will achieve social peace and well-being, without abandoning the organization of their life for the purpose of personal gain, which is the cause of war. So, when they are confronted by industrial disputes, they seek busily to improvise expedients for securing a new balance of power, or even appeal to the State to enforce a settlement, as though the absence of a principle could be compensated by machinery. But in fact no such expedients exist. Combatants may be willing to surrender their own interests to a principle or cause or institution superior to them both, as soldiers, to use Ruskin's example, are willing to be killed for the service of their country. But they will not surrender them to each other, any more than soldiers would consent to be killed for the personal profit of their officers; and when a society by precept and practice has fostered the doctrine that its foundation is the pursuit of personal pecuniary advantage, it will not be able to appeal to men to forego that advantage when it happens to find the application of the doctrine inconvenient.

If the classes who have controlled it desire to retain the joys of self-aggrandisement, they cannot demand from others the virtues of self-renunciation. If men have been taught that the whole meaning of economic activity is to accumulate profits for a private employer, they are not likely to listen—why should they?—when they are told that they ought to show a tender solicitude for the interest of the community. And if there is no principle which determines what each group should justly get, then it is idle for the public to complain if each group organizes itself to get what it can.

Ruskin thought that there was such a principle, that men should be paid for the service and service only, 'that the usurer's trade will be abolished utterly; that the employer will be paid justly for his superintendence, but not for his capital; and the landlord paid for his superintendence of the cultivation of land, when he is able to direct it wisely'. He advised men to achieve peace, not by seeking peace, but by seeking to serve a common end, and organizing their industry for the attainment of that end and that alone.

PART II
EDUCATION

4

KEEP THE WORKERS' CHILDREN
IN THEIR PLACE[1]

While the nation as a whole has seen in the Education Bill[2] the tentative beginnings of a new and more humane educational policy, there are those to whom the subordination of education to economic exigencies is still, apparently, an indisputable axiom. It would be unfair, no doubt, to attach too much weight to the Memorandum on Education recently issued by the Education Committee of the Federation of British Industries. Both in and out of the Federation there are a considerable number of employers to whom its naïve materialism will be highly uncongenial.

But the document is significant as the expression of a point of view which, though it is not representative, is not deterred by any false modesty from desiring to appear so, and which aims at intimidating the Government into abandoning the central element in its educational programme by the suggestion that the big battalions of industry have put their foot down. In thus attempting to mobilize the business interests against the children, the Federation of British Industries has unintentionally rendered a genuine service to the cause of educational reform. For it has revealed the motive and social policy which lie behind the opposition to the extension of higher education. They have only to be stated, in order to be rejected decisively by the public opinion of the community.

The days when education could be resisted by a direct frontal attack have passed, and the Education Committee of the Federation of British Industries is good enough to begin its Memorandum by assuring the public that it yearns for 'an

[1] Article appearing in the *Daily News*, 14.2.1918.
[2] Leading to the 'Fisher' Education Act of 1918, which abolished all exemption from school attendance for children under fourteen, extended public provision for higher education, and proposed a system of compulsory 'continuation schools'.

47

improvement of the education system'. But it contrives, when it comes to the consideration of particular measures of educational reform, successfully to dissemble the affection which it feels for reform in the abstract. In particular, while it dwells on the need for better elementary education, and speaks feelingly of secondary education for 'the more able children', and demands a better system of training for teachers, it cannot accept the proposal which is the heart and kernel of the present Education Bill. Indeed, at the mere suggestion that all young persons should spend a small part of their time upon higher education, it cries and cuts itself with knives, quite like a person who is not fired by a passion for educational progress.

The Federation's first objection to the Education Bill is that unlimited supplies of juvenile labour are indispensable to industry, and that the proposals of that arch-Bolshevik, Mr Fisher, will shake to its foundations the fragile fabric of British industrial prosperity. 'A period of eight hours a week taken out of working hours would impose a burden upon many industries which they would be *quite unable to bear*, except as a process of very gradual development.'

Now it is true, of course, that any extension of education involves some industrial readjustment. It is also true that the lamentations of a certain section of employers over the prospective ruin of British industry have been part of the ritual which has accompanied the passage of every Education Act since 1870, and of every Factory Act since 1802; that experience has refuted these predictions as regularly as ignorance has made them; and that the 'burden' imposed by the present measure is insignificant compared with that borne by French and German employers before the war in the shape of military conscription. To suggest that British industry is suspended over an abyss by a slender thread of juvenile labour, which eight hours continued education will snap, that after a century of scientific discovery and economic progress it is still upon the bent backs of children of fourteen that our industrial organization, and national prosperity, and that rare birth of time, the Federation of British Industries itself, repose—is not all this, after all, a little pitiful?

After fifty years of practical experience of the effort of raising the age of school attendance, the onus of proof rests upon those who allege that education will impede industry, not upon those who argue that education will stimulate all healthy national activities, and industry among them. Nevertheless, it may very readily be conceded that the establishment of a system of continued education from fourteen to eighteen will involve, like all other reforms, some practical difficulties. Very well, then; the Federation consists of practical men, to whom the nation may naturally appeal for assistance in overcoming them. What help do they offer?

They offer, apparently, none. While well-known leaders of the cotton industry have been at pains to suggest how the circumstances of their particular trade might be adapted to meet the principle of the Education Bill, the attitude adopted in the Memorandum of the Federation of British Industries is one of frigid opposition to the whole policy of universal continued education. Education, it states, ought not to be extended beyond fourteen, 'until . . . the labour market has adjusted itself to the new conditions'. Of any consciousness, as is felt by an increasing number of employers, that there is an obligation upon those who organize industry to take pains to adapt it to the requirements of education, of any suspicion that fifty-five and a half to sixty hours' labour a week may actually be excessive for children who have just left school, or that to stop education abruptly at fourteen is to stop it when it is just beginning to be most fruitful, or that there is a duty to the higher education to build a better world for all, there is, in this precious document, not a trace. The Bourbons of industry who drafted it have learned nothing and forgotten nothing. Europe is in ruins; and out of the sea of blood and tears the Federation of British Industries emerges jaunty and unabashed, clamouring that whatever else is shaken, the vested interest of employers in the labour of children of fourteen must not be disturbed by so much as eight hours a week.

But it is not merely for economic reasons that the Federation is opposed to higher education for all young persons. It is absolved from the necessity of proving that universal higher education is impossible because it does not really believe that universal higher education is desirable. Behind the objection based on the convenience of industry lies another objection based on the theory that all except a small minority of children

49

are incapable of benefiting by education beyond the age of fourteen. It is not actually stated, indeed, that working-class children, like anthropoid apes, have fewer convolutions in their brains than the children of captains of industry. But the authors of the Memorandum are evidently sceptical as to either the possibility or the desirability of offering higher education to more than a small proportion of them.

In the manner of a European traveller describing a race which is too backward to count up to more than ten, it draws a sharp distinction between 'the more promising' child who is mentally capable of benefiting by higher education, and 'the less promising' child who is not. For the former there is to be full-time secondary education. For the latter there is to be elementary education up to fourteen, part of which, in the last two years of school life—a sinister suggestion—'might be directly vocational and intended to fit the child for the particular industry which he will enter at fourteen'; and then full-time work in the factory. Nor is it contemplated that the children who are 'mentally capable of profiting by secondary education' will be more than a select minority. In a charming sentence, which reveals in a flash the view which it takes both of the function of the working classes in society and of the meaning of education, the Memorandum enters a solemn caveat against the dangers of excessive education. 'They would very strongly advise that in selecting children for higher education, care should be taken to avoid creating, as was done, for example, in India, a large class of persons *whose education is unsuitable for the employment which they eventually enter.*'

There it is, the whole Master Class theory of society in a sentence! One cannot refute it by argument, as one can refute the Federation's particular prophecies of the industrial disaster which would be caused by a more general diffusion of higher education. For this is not a question of fact, but of ultimate beliefs, and those who think that men are first of all men have no premise in common with those who think, like the authors of the Federation's Memorandum, that they are first of all servants, or animals, or tools.

One cannot, I say, disprove such a doctrine, any more than one can disprove a taste for militarism, or for drugs, or for bad novels. But one can expose its consequences. And its consequences are simple. They are some new form of slavery. Stripped of its decent draperies of convention, what it means is that education is to be used, not to enable human beings to become themselves through the development of their personalities, nor to strengthen the spirit of social solidarity, nor to prepare men for the better service of their fellows, nor to raise the general level of society; but to create a new commercial aristocracy, based on the selection for higher education of 'the more promising' children of working-class parents from among the vulgar mass, who are fit only to serve as the cannon-fodder of capitalist industry.

This, then, is the subtle discovery which, as they pore over the lessons of the past three years, inspires in the Federation of British Industries bright hopes of a more profitable future. There are classes who are ends and classes who are means—upon that grand original distinction the community is invited to base its educational system. The aim of education is to reflect, to defend, and to perpetuate the division of mankind into masters and servants. How delicate an insight into the relative value of human beings and of material riches! How generous a heritage into which to welcome the children of men who fell in the illusion that, in their humble way, they were the servants of freedom!

But why has the Federation reserved these revelations till now? If its gospel had been before the world in August, 1914, it might have reconciled us to the Prussian Government, which has long appreciated and practised it. Much money and several lives, both 'more promising' and 'less promising'—though perhaps the latter are hardly worth considering—might have been saved. As it is, it is just three-and-a-half years too late. The Federation must try again. And before it does so, let it read and digest the remark of Bacon: 'The Blessings of Judah and Issachar will never meet, that the same people shall be a lion's whelp and an ass between burdens.'

5

THE PROBLEM OF THE PUBLIC SCHOOLS[1]

I. THE LEGACY OF THE LAST CENTURY

The view sometimes heard that 'the public school system'[2] is hallowed by antiquity is a piece of mythology. Particular institutions can point to links with the past of somewhat the kind as exist between the city companies of today and mediaeval craft-gilds. These pedigrees, dignified or picturesque, are not without their education value; but a long boarding-school tradition does not often form part of them. In reality, the assumption still prevalent among well-to-do parents in England —an assumption not countenanced by the most eminent of the founders of modern public-school education—that residence for four or five years at a boarding-school should form, as a matter of course, a stage in the life of all boys above a certain income level, together with the existence of a group of schools which specialize in catering for that demand, are, on anything like their present scale, a thing of yesterday. Individual specimens both of the attitude and of the institution are to be encountered much earlier; but 'the public-school system', in so far as these are its characteristics, has no long history behind it. It represents, in its present form, not an ancient educational tradition, but innovations which matured between 1830 and 1890.

The reasons which made these two generations the golden

---

[1] First appeared as an article in the *Political Quarterly*, April/June, 1943; later printed as a WEA pamphlet.
[2] British 'public schools' are, of course, anything but public. They are private, fee-paying schools. What entitles them to recognition as 'public schools' is the purely empirical test of whether or not they are members of the Head Masters' Conference. These schools are of various types; some residential, some day-schools. In this paper, Tawney is concerned mainly with the boarding-schools. They present, he says, 'the more difficult problem'.—Editor.

age of the public boarding-school are not difficult to state. The moral authority and practical example of pioneers, such as Arnold and Thring, were of great importance; but conditions peculiar to their day fixed the direction of their efforts, and it is no reflection on their originality to say that, even more than most successful reformers, they worked with the grain. Apart from the influence of individuals, the decisive factors were four. They were the Industrial Revolution, with its flood of new wealth; the deficiencies, both in number and quality, of existing day-schools; the modernization of communications; and the careers opened by the expansion of the empire, the reform of the civil service and the growth of the professions. The first greatly increased the effective demand for high secondary education. The second and third put a premium on boarding-schools and made recourse to them practicable. The fourth ensured that the aptitudes cultivated by them would find little difficulty, when school-days were over, in securing suitable employment.

The rising middle class, if often uneducated itself, was not unaware of the advantages of education; nor was it lacking in ambition. It looked to the schools to provide, in addition to a moral and intellectual discipline, a common platform enabling its sons to associate on equal terms with those of families who, if thoroughly out-distanced in income, still diffused a faint aroma of social superiority. At first, it looked in vain. The old local foundations were often in ruins. The local secondary schools of today were not yet even a dream. The condition of not a few private schools was such that the choice, parents were told by one with some title to speak, 'lies between public schools and an education whose character may be strictly . . . domestic'.[1] If they rejected the last course, what alternative had they but to send their sons to schools at a distance from their homes? Yet how, in the days when Arnold himself travelled to his new post at Rugby by stage-coach, and despatched his belongings by the Grand Junction Canal, could the first alternative be generally adopted?

The answer came, not from the educationalist, but from the engineer. It is not an accident that the boarding-school boom

[1] A. P. Stanley, *The Life and Correspondence of Thomas Arnold*, p. 242 (Minerva Library ed.).

followed closely on a railway boom, that three times as many public schools were founded in the thirty years between 1841 and 1871 as in the whole country before 1841, and that enterprising grammar schools made haste to fall in with the fashion, sometimes placating their consciences for the diversion of their services from day-boys to boarders by supporting cheap day-schools for the sons of local residents. A form of education which improved communications made possible was made increasingly attractive by the requirements of a state beginning tardily to grapple with the problems of an empire and an urban civilization. The establishment in 1854 of open competition as the condition of entry to the Indian Civil Service, the application of the same principle to the Home Civil Service between 1855 and 1870, and the gradual assumption by governments of functions demanding an enlarged administrative personnel, combined with the growth of law, medicine and business to create a market in which, before the days of municipal and county secondary schools, the products of the public schools for long met few competitors. Parents with means were quick to grasp the advantages of the new dispensation. It could be said by a headmaster in the early seventies not only that the 'ordinary English gentleman would think that he lost caste' if he did not send his boy to a public school, but that 'there is a strong feeling growing up among the merchant class in favour of the public schools, and (that) hundreds go to a school now who, thirty years ago, would not have thought of doing so'.[1]

Every stage of education casts its influence back, for good or evil, on that preceding it. It is not surprising, therefore, that the first preparatory school of the modern type should have been founded, apparently, on the suggestion of Arnold. The increase in the number of such schools from something under a score in the sixties to approximately four hundred in 1900 supplied the public boarding-schools with a *clientèle* of the social type which they desired, educated under conditions not dissimilar from their own. It is a commonplace that England possesses, not one educational system, but two—a public and a private one. At the close of the century, the former was still in an early stage of its history; the latter was not far from complete.

[1] G. P. Parkin, *Edward Thring, Life, Diary and Letters*, II, pp. 195–196.

The 'public school system' of today, therefore, in so far as it is represented by the great boarding-schools, is not among the more venerable of the historic treasures of the English people. It grew to maturity between the first and third Reform Acts, as the child of a particular age and a specific environment. Like the reorganization of local government and the changes which followed the first Royal Commission on Oxford and Cambridge, it was one phase of the great movement of middle-class reconstruction which began in 1832, reached its climax in the eighties, and then, its impetus spent, settled down to make the most of the kingdom it had won, leaving, as was inevitable, new tasks to be essayed by novel methods and in a spirit not its own.

No student of English life in the latter half of the last century will question the magnitude of the improvements in the education of the propertied and professional classes which were gathering way. No fair-minded critic, whatever his own sympathies, will depreciate the beneficial effects which those improvements produced, not only on those who directly experienced them, but on the nation as a whole. The most enlightened of reformers, however, must work with the materials to his hand; and the public boarding-schools, whether reconstituted or newly founded, took, for good and for evil, the stamp of their day. The better among them owed much, and added much, to the practical energy, the admirable moral seriousness, the respect for the hard grind of the intellect, without fancies or frills, of Victorian England. All of them, including the best, were impoverished by the feebleness of the social spirit of the same England. All of them were the victims of its precipitous class divisions, its dreary cult of gentility, its inability to conceive of education as the symbol and cement of a spiritual unity transcending differences of birth and wealth.

Two features of the period, in particular, condemned those schools to a position which they could hardly, at the time—even had they wished it—have avoided, but which later were to prove both mischievous to the nation and humiliating to them. Since no public system of education existed, in which they could take their place, they came to form, as they rose in number and influence, a separate order of their own. They developed, not as partners in a community of educational effort, welcoming the obligations which such partnership imposes and zealous to bring their contributions to the common stock, but as the apostles of an exaggerated individualism, which, at first, perhaps, was inevitable, but which survived into an age when it was no longer a necessity forced upon them by the backwardness of public education, but a cherished idiosyncracy. Isolated from what were to be the main streams of the nation's educational life, and flattered by the eminent, they were under strong inducements to become the egoists of the educational world, whose pride in the uniqueness of their excellences was stronger than their eagerness to share them. It cannot be said that they have been notably successful in resisting that temptation.

Since, in the second place, there was no question in their seminal period of state grants to secondary education, the public boarding-schools were compelled, unless blessed with endowments, to finance themselves from fees; and their wares, being expensive, had to be sold in a market in which price was a secondary consideration. Here again, at first, they had no alternative; and, here again, till recently, they do not seem to have sought one. Towards the end of the decade of rapid educational development which followed the Act of 1902, it was suggested by a headmaster that the public schools should accept state-aid and public supervision, in order both to improve the quality of their education and to reduce its cost. It may be doubted whether the Government of the day would have smiled on that proposal; but, while the number of day-schools on the grant-list has steadily increased, and included in 1938 some sixty-five public schools, the public boarding-schools, as far as known to the writer, took at the time no step in that direction. Their social character was already fixed, and history was too strong for them. They had grown up as the servants, not of the nation, but of one small stratum within it. Their pupils, their staffs, their governing bodies, were drawn from a single class. The conversion of a luxury trade for the well-to-do into one supplying a less select *clientèle* is never an easy undertaking. Either the schools concerned did not make the effort, or it proved beyond their power.

II. THE CASE FOR REFORM

'The public schools,' observed in 1909 Dr Norwood and Mr Hope, 'generally produce a race of well-bodied, well-mannered, well-meaning boys, keen at games, devoted to their schools, ignorant of life, contemptuous of all outside the pale of their own caste, uninterested in work, neither desiring or revering knowledge . . . A sound economy of finance would certainly result in a considerable reduction in the cost of a public-school training, to the advantage both of the often sorely-taxed parent and of the public schools themselves, since they would gain in usefulness what they lost in exclusiveness.'[1] There is reason to believe that the intellectual standards of all or most public schools have improved out of recognition in the last thirty years. With higher salary scales, better staffing ratios, and more ample provision of amenities, than most grant-aided secondary schools have been in a position to afford, they have been able to offer an education at once more intensive and more diversified than has hitherto been practicable in the majority of the latter. Good judges have paid tribute to the high quality of their educational work. It is probable that, were the authors of *Higher Education of Boys in England* writing today, their strictures on the mental stagnation of public-school boys would be omitted or much modified.

That point should be emphasized, especially by a critic, both on grounds of justice and because it is obviously important that reform, whatever shape it may assume, should not impair educational values, but should preserve them and extend their influence. It cannot be said with equal confidence, however, that the social idiosyncrasies of the schools in question have followed the contempt for knowledge into the limbo of the past. On the prevalence of the 'caste' spirit, views, doubtless, will differ, though it is significant that observers from the Dominions and the United States—not to mention Scandinavia and France—are not slow to detect its presence and to lift their eyebrows at it. 'Exclusiveness', of which that spirit is the natural product, is a matter, not of opinion, but of fact. It is

[1] Norwood and Hope, *The Higher Education of Boys in England*, pp. 187 and 189.

mitigated, of course by scholarships and concessions to parents, which, though rarely of benefit to the children of wage-earners, play a valuable part in lightening the educational burdens of middle-class families. Subject to that qualification, the select character of the more expensive boarding-schools, which in the eyes of their feebler-minded clients is not the least among their assets, is maintained by a scale of fees which automatically restricts their use to the relatively well-to-do. They are, in fact, public schools from which the children of the great majority of the public are rigorously excluded.

In such circumstances, the statement that they are class institutions cannot seriously be contested. The apologist who emphasizes the variety of occupational groups represented by the parents sending sons to these schools, and who applauds the liberal spirit which they have shown in admitting the sons of 'dentists, bank-managers, and the more successful shop-keepers',[1] is, doubtless, correct. But he confirms, rather than invalidates, the charge of exclusiveness. Approximately three-quarters of the occupied population consist of wage-earners. What proportion do the sons of wage-earners form of the pupils to be found in the more expensive schools? The Committee of the Headmasters' Conference deprecates, in another connection, the creation of 'an impassable gulf separating the schools of the wealthy from the schools of the poor'.[2] To the ordinary man who looks at Eton, or Harrow or Winchester, or a dozen other celebrated schools, it is precisely such a gulf that appears to exist today.

Educational policy is always social policy. In the England of the later nineteenth century, when the public school system was in the making, it could plausibly be argued that the recruitment of educational institutions on the basis of wealth, if in itself unedifying, was not out of tune with the temper of the day. In their subservience to money and social position, and the tranquil, unsophisticated class-consciousness which that subservience bred, the public boarding-schools, it might be said, did not rise above the standards of their generation, but neither did they fall below them. Their virtues were genuine and their own; their vices were of a piece with those of the

[1] *The Political Quarterly*, July–September, 1943.
[2] *Public Schools and the Future* (Headmasters' Conference, August, 1943), p. 27.

society about them. Whether convincing, or not, in the past, that defence is clearly out of date.

Since the public school system assumed its present shape, England has become a political democracy. The public boarding-schools continue to serve much the same tiny class as in the days when Lord Balfour was at Eton and Lord Baldwin at Harrow. A national system of education has not only been created in the interval, but has revealed unanticipated possibilities of growth. It is hardly an exaggeration to say that, as far as the contact with it of the great majority of the public boarding-schools goes, it might as well not exist. Institutions so immune to the stresses and demands of a changing environment may enjoy some of the advantages of an old *régime*, but they suffer also from its weaknesses. It is not primarily a question of the attitude of headmasters, or even of governing bodies; for representative figures among the former have expressed themselves strongly, if with reservations, in favour of reform, and the latter, however opaque their prejudices, could not prevent it, once it had become the national policy. It is a question of the reluctance of a small, but influential, class to acquiesce in interference with institutions which it has come to regard as peculiarly its own; of its fears of the keener competition for posts of profit and distinction which will result from a diminution of educational inequalities; of a temper which values the more exclusive public schools, not only as organs of culture, but as instruments of power; of public indifference; of the refusal of Governments, for each and all of these reasons, to take a thorny subject up. As a consequence the public boarding-schools have been permitted to live in isolation from the educational needs of the mass of the population and from the system which serves them. What are the results of that policy?

(1) Its first result is obvious. The rising generation is submitted in youth to a somewhat rigid system of educational segregation, which is also a system of social segregation. Whether Disraeli's famous epigram is still applicable or not to the adult population, it certainly remains true of the young, though, thanks to the development of public education, it is less true than in the recent past. Given the existing economic order, sharp class divisions exist independently of educational

organization and policy. It is unreasonable, therefore, to speak of the public boarding-schools as creating them. But education ought to be solvent of such divisions. It is difficult to deny that the tendency of those schools is to deepen and perpetuate them. 'The very existence of the public schools, as they now are,' writes Mr Simpson, himself formerly a master at one of them, 'helps to keep the different social classes ignorant of one another, and aggravates misunderstanding to an extent which public school men commonly do not realize.'[1] Is it possible convincingly to challenge that criticism?

There is something to be said for preserving some schools only loosely connected with the national educational system, on the ground that their existence is favourable to initiative, experiment, and diversity of educational type. There is nothing whatever to be said for preserving schools whose distinctive characteristic is that they are recruited almost exclusively from the children of parents with larger incomes than their neighbours. That infliction on the young of the remorseless rigours of the economic calculus is mischievous for two reasons. It is unfair to them, and it is injurious to society. Children learn from each other more than the most skilful of masters can teach them. Easy, natural and unself-conscious contacts between young people of varying traditions and different social background are not the least valuable part of their education. They are not only a stimulating influence in youth, but the best preparation for an attitude which makes the most of life in later years. An educational system which discourages them is, to that extent, not a good system, but a bad one.

The predominantly one-class school is not favourable to them. Not only is an obvious injustice done when children are excluded by financial barriers from the schools in question, but the pupils admitted to them are themselves injured. They are taught, not in words or of set purpose, but by the mere facts of their environment, that they are members, in virtue of the family bank-account, of a privileged group, whose function it will be, on however humble a scale, to direct and command, and to which leadership, influence, and the other prizes of life properly belong. The capacity of youth to protect itself against the imbecilities of its elders is not the least among

[1] J. H. Simpson, *The Future of the Public Schools.*

the graces bestowed on it by Heaven; but that does not excuse us for going out of our way gratuitously to inflict our fatuities upon it. If some of the victims continue throughout life, as unhappily they do, to see the world through class spectacles, a policy which insists on their wearing them at school must bear part of the responsibility. Insolence and servility in the old may well be incurable, and are a subject for pity rather than for indignation. But why persist in transmitting the bacilli to the young?

Nor, of course, is it only individuals who suffer from our erection of educational snobbery into a national institution. The nation, as a whole, pays a heavy price for it. The complicated business of democratic government demands, with the world as it is, a high capacity of co-operation; and co-operation, in its turn, depends on mutual understanding. A common educational background fosters such understanding. An organization of education which treats different sections of the population as though they belonged to different species is an impediment to it. It is precisely such a treatment which is our present practice. Its effects on public life are heightened, of course, by other factors, but they remain only too visible.

The higher ranges of the British Civil Service have many virtues. What too frequently they lack is not intelligence, or expert knowledge, or public spirit, or devotion to duty. It is personal experience of the conditions of life and habits of thought of those for whose requirements in the matter of health, housing, education and economic well-being, they are engaged in providing. That deficiency is serious. Yet how, as long as the schools attended by a somewhat high proportion of the individuals concerned are schools which no common child can enter, can they be blamed for suffering from it?

There is no reason to suppose that the personnel of the British diplomatic service does not possess the same virtues in abundance. If, nevertheless, some of its members surprise friendly foreign observers by their inability to mix on easy terms with any but small cliques, the reason is partly the same. It is commonly not, as their exasperated critics are apt to complain, that they are swollen with British arrogance, but that they have been immolated in youth on the altar of good form. They have breathed at school the close atmosphere of a social sect, whose conventions they have learned to regard as the right thing. Too often they continue to mistake the provincialisms of a class for the interests and manners of civilized mankind. The mood of nervous defensiveness revealed by some, though, of course not by all, of the spokesmen of the public boarding-schools at the prospect of a large influx of pupils of a different stamp—as though these harmless young people were a species of sub-boy, some few of whose members can be domesticated, but most are to be shunned—is a third illustration, at once comic and sad, of the artificial ignorance engendered by our educational divisions. Must we really regard as the last word in wisdom arrangements which cause able and amiable men to shrink in alarm from contact with their fellow-countrymen?

The co-existence of a public and a private educational system is not without influence on Parliament itself. It causes the economic lines between parties to coincide in large measure with educational lines. Such a coincidence is on all grounds unfortunate. It means that education, which should be the great uniter, becomes itself a ground of division, and that not a few members, even when they themselves have no interest at stake, approach questions of importance to the mass of their fellow-countrymen in a spirit, if not of hostility, of insolent indifference, which would hardly be possible had they and their opponents rubbed shoulders at school up to sixteen or eighteen. That spirit is apt to be seen at its worst when education itself is under discussion. Members who have served on Local Education Authorities can usually be relied on, irrespective of party, to show sense and good feeling; they have seen the children and succumbed to them. Too many of the remainder—to judge by their behaviour—find it difficult to believe that the children of common persons are human in quite the same sense as their own. They have rarely themselves been educated in schools which are directly affected by parliamentary decisions on educational policy, nor do they often send their sons to them. They can hardly be expected—apart, of course, from bright exceptions—to regard the improvement of those schools as the urgent issue which it is. On any sane view, the preparation of the young for life is among the greatest of common interests. When the economic divisions of the adult world are allowed to reproduce themselves in the educational system, it is difficult for that truism to win general recognition. Thus the evil legacy perpetuates itself.

(2) The resources of character and capacity at the disposal of the nation, though far larger than are utilized at present, are not unlimited. The course of wisdom for it, therefore, is to make certain of turning to the best account as much of both as it commands. It is to encourage an easy movement of ability to the types of education best calculated to cultivate it, and an easy movement, again, from educational institutions to the posts which such ability is qualified to fill. *La carrière ouverte aux talents*—promotion by merit—is neither the sole object of educational policy nor, in the view of the writer, the most important one; but it is clearly an object which should be given its due weight. The immense tasks which confront the nation during the coming generation enhance its significance.

Success in attaining that end depends on the general educational and social policy of a country, not on any particular group of schools. But all schools should co-operate, according to their opportunities, in facilitating its attainment, and none should thwart or ignore it. The existence of schools recruited primarily by an income test obstructs it in two ways. It results, in the first place, in the misdirection of ability. The children of parents of small means, whatever their natural aptitudes for the types of education which the public boarding-schools provide, are prevented by their cost from obtaining access to them. The children of the well-to-do are not infrequently sent to such schools on account of the social prestige which they confer, even when they would benefit more by an education of a different sort. Education maladjustments of the kind are unjust to individuals and injurious to the nation. They prevent it from making the best use of the talents at its disposal.

The second effect of a system of selection for higher education in which, not merely the personal qualities of the young, but the financial means of their parents, play a determining part, is equally serious. It is unduly to narrow the area from which recruits for positions of responsibility are drawn in later life. It is sometimes said that the peculiar function of the public boarding-schools is to 'educate for leadership', and that the social life which they offer specially fits them for that task. All schools, elementary, secondary, and the particular species of secondary schools called 'public', have produced leaders; and it may readily be admitted that, for reasons which are not difficult to state, the last has hitherto contributed more than its fair quota. But, before the claim can be conceded in the form in which it is sometimes advanced, two considerations must be weighed.

In the first place, there is no such thing as leadership in the abstract. The qualities needed by a leader depend on the social environment in which he works, on the nature of the problems that he is called upon to solve, and not least—if his *métier* is government—on the political psychology of those who are to be led. All three have changed profoundly, both at home and abroad, in the last half-century, nor is there any probability that that process will be arrested. The truth is that leadership demands different gifts at different periods, and that no formula for producing it can be other than provisional. There are times—to refer only to politics—when the even-handed justice of an authoritarian government provides an adequate answer to most situations. There are others when a kindly paternalism is less important than the capacity to co-operate, in a spirit of equality, with all sorts and conditions of men, irrespective of differences of class, colour and creed. There are others, again, when a habit of benevolent superiority is a ruinous liability, and when leadership involves an ability to sympathize with popular movements, and a sufficient interest in the economic and technical conditions of social progress, to be qualified to play an active part in promoting it. A nation which intends to hold its own in the world must take account of such changing requirements and play to the score. It may well be the case that the characteristics alleged—often, doubtless with truth—to be fostered by a public boarding-school were a not too inadequate equipment for certain kinds of leadership in the past. But is it so certain that they remain adequate today, or that, if they do, a secondary day-school is incapable of cultivating them?

In order, in the second place, that an institution may be successful in training leaders, it is not enough that it should provide an education well suited for that purpose; it is necessary also that it should cast its net wide. The way to pick a strong team of athletes is not to exclude from it everyone with less than £10 a week, but to consider all candidates for inclusion, irrespective of their economic circumstances, and then to choose them on their merits. The way to encourage able leadership whether in scholarship and science, politics or economic life is, in principle, the same. If a school begins by ruling out as ineligible all potential leaders who cannot satisfy an exacting income test, the individuals on whom it lavishes its skill will not be those best qualified to lead, but only—a very different thing—those best qualified among the small minority who alone can comply with that initial requirement. Of course, if it is content merely to count among its old boys men who, for one reason or another, have reached positions of prominence, then money and social influence have hitherto been good horses to back. But that version of the venerable pastime of spotting the winner can hardly be intended, when the public boarding-schools are praised as the nurseries of the nation's leaders.

In reality, education for leadership especially in a democracy, is not a simple matter. It is a question, not only of intensive cultivation, but of a wide range of selection; not only of the education of pupils actually admitted to schools, but of the principles determining the admission of some and the exclusion of others. It is likely to be a success when the right kind of education is easily accessible to those best qualified to profit by it. When such education is surrounded by high financial hedges, the education itself may still be good, but, as an aid to the production of able leadership, it is likely to be a failure.

Considered from that point of view, the limitations of the English educational system appear somewhat serious. No adequate statistical evidence exists showing the schools from which persons eminent in different walks of life are drawn; nor in the nature of things, can such evidence be up-to-date. Such scraps of information, however, as are available suggest that Great Britain draws on the capacity of all its citizens to a less degree than do, for example, the United States and the Dominions, and that leadership in politics, administration and finance is recruited—less exclusively, indeed, than in the past, but still predominantly—not from the population as a whole but from the small circle of families—perhaps 3 per cent of the nation—who can afford to pay for an expensive education. In the words of the *Economist*,[1] 'the public schools turn out, perhaps, 10,000 boys a year; from this tiny fraction we select the great majority of those who are to be given an easy road to the top. The selection is clearly not one of merit.' Here, again, the primary responsibility is less that of the schools concerned than of a public which is at once indulgent to educational privilege and parsimonious in providing for the adequate development of secondary education. The consequences of its attitude are, however, somewhat serious. A nation which permits the continuance of the state of things described by the *Economist* is grappling with its problems with one hand tied behind its back.

(3) If an educational system is to mobilize its full power, it is not sufficient that each of the institutions composing it should make the most of its own virtues without regard to the remainder. It is necessary that all of them should play their varying roles as conscious partners in a common effort. The pedantries of over-organization are, of course, to be avoided; but so also is a selfish or capricious individualism. There should be a general recognition that, while a good school is a community with distinctive characteristics, every school has responsibilities, not merely to its immediate *clientèle*, but to the nation as a whole; and such a relation should exist between all schools and the State so as to ensure that those responsibilities are not ignored. It is not a question of mechanical systematization, but of co-operation within a framework which finds room for wide diversities of educational type, but ensures that such diversities contribute to the common end of an educated nation.

If, judged by that standard, the public boarding-schools of today leave something to be desired, it is history, rather than any wilful perversity, which must be regarded as the culprit. Most of them were firmly established at a time when public education was still in its infancy. But a position of isolation, which was inevitable in the past, is unnecessary today, and, being needless, has become mischievous. Unfortunately, it still continues. The schools in question touch the public educational system at its apex, through their connection with the universities; but, being fed by expensive preparatory schools, they are

[1] *The Economist*, November 23, 1940.

66

rarely in touch with its lower ranges. Receiving, in most cases, no grants, they are not subject to the secondary regulations of the Board, and their contacts with it are at present confined to the voluntary acceptance of inspection by its officials. Between them and the Local Education Authorities, with their six million children and quarter of a million or so teachers, direct contacts hardly exist. The team-spirit which leads individuals to play for their side rather than for themselves, is commonly counted among the public school virtues. It cannot be said that those schools themselves are a shining example of it. Like the Cyclops, 'each governs his own children, nor do they trouble about their neighbours'.

That state of things is not confined to the public boarding-schools. It is a particular case of the general problem arising from the existence of a multitude of private schools, with which no public authority has power to interfere. Its disadvantages are somewhat serious. If the nation is to make the most effective use of its educational resources, it must be in a position to bring them all under review, and to act on the conclusions which a comprehensive survey suggests. As long as one small group of important schools, and many thousand schools of inferior standing, are completely or predominantly outside the purview of the Board and the Local Education Authorities, such action is impossible. That situation is unfortunate, whatever the view taken of the merits or demerits of residential education. It is conceivable that the number of boarding-schools is excessive, and that some of them would be of greater service if converted into day-schools. No public authority has power to reduce it, or even to prevent the foundation of additional schools of the same type. It is conceivable, on the other hand, that the number of boarding-schools is deficient, and ought to be increased; but to increase it solely with the purpose of meeting the needs of those children who cannot afford to enter existing schools would be to perpetuate the very cleavage based on wealth which it is important to overcome. Here again, therefore, if an addition to boarding-school provision is thought to be desirable, what is needed is to plan that provision as a whole, and to ensure that boys pass to the schools, whether to be established in future or already in existence, for which they are best suited, without their choice being biased by financial considerations.

And here, again, no authority exists with power to do anything of the kind.

It is clearly desirable, in the second place, that the arrangements as to the admission of pupils to different types of secondary schools should be sufficiently similar not to impose needless obstacles on the entry of boys suited for this type or that. The fact that one group of schools is private, and another public, makes a reasonable measure of co-operation needlessly difficult of attainment. Other things being equal, diversity of social and educational experience in teaching staffs, and the easy movement of teachers between schools of different types, are an asset. Both tend to be discouraged by the same sharp cleavage.

Sympathy is naturally evoked by the claim of schools for freedom to develop each its own special *ethos* and educational methods. Matters of school government and finance, however, including, where they exist, endowments and the management of boarding-houses, stand in a different category. It is not satisfactory that governing bodies should be as heavily weighted as some are at present with decorative notabilities, to the exclusion of under-representation of public education authorities; or that fees and other costs which have risen greatly in the course of the last generation, should be subject to no form of public control; or that no public authority should be responsible for seeing that the domestic economy of public boarding-schools —an aspect of school life which is not, after all, the speciality of teachers—is conducted on modern lines, and with reasonable regard to economy and efficiency. It is probable that, as far as matters of this kind are concerned, not only the public, but the schools themselves, have everything to gain from the pressure of a central authority which can pool the experience of a number of different institutions, and correct individual aberrations or laxities by reference to a range of knowledge which no single one of them can command.

The fundamental issue is simple. It is whether the existence of a group of schools reserved for the children of the comparatively prosperous, and in a large measure isolated from the public system of education, is or is not, as the world is today, in the best interests of the nation. It cannot be decided by the venerable device of describing privileges as liberties. Educational freedom, like other kinds of freedom, does not consist in the right of every individual to use such economic advantages as he may happen to possess in order to secure special opportunities for himself and his children, or in the unfettered discretion of those who control educational resources to employ them, if they think fit, to gratify that natural, but anti-social, egotism. It is a reality in so far as, and only in so far as, education is organized in such a manner as to enable all, whatever their economic circumstances, to make the most of the powers with which they are endowed. No single group of institutions can make more than a small contribution to that end. It is none the less its duty, and should be its pride, to contribute to it what it can.

The England of the next twenty years will not be a nest of singing-birds. Those who guide the nation's schools can do more than is given to most men to create the common culture which at present we lack. To serve educational needs, without regard to the vulgar irrelevancies of class and income, is part of the teacher's honour. Schools claiming to represent the best that English secondary education has to show should be the first to offer an example of that spirit.

6

AN EXPERIMENT IN DEMOCRATIC
EDUCATION[1]

I. THE IDEA

It is surely a very barren kind of pedantry which would treat
education as though it were a closed compartment within
which principles are developed and experiments tried undisturbed by the changing social currents of the world around.
The truth is that educational problems cannot be considered
in isolation from the aspirations of the great bodies of men and
women for whose sake alone it is that educational problems are
worth considering at all.

The way in which the educational policy of a period reflects
its conceptions of human society and of the proper object of
human endeavour is well illustrated by the part which has in
the past been played, and is still played today, by two ideas,
the idea of status and the idea of the career open to talent. The
former would adjust the character and duration of education
in rough accordance with the social class of those for whom
education is being provided. The latter would qualify the
resultant rigidity of social stratification by creating special
machinery to enable intellect to climb from one stratum to
another. The first gave us the early elementary schools, in
which the 'labouring poor' were to acquire learning 'suitable to
their status'. The second was a potent force behind the reform of
the older universities in the middle of the nineteenth century, and
has influenced in varying degrees more recent scholarship systems.

Historically opposed on many a ringing field, they are both

[1] First appeared in *The Political Quarterly*, May, 1914; later reprinted as a pamphlet
by the WEA. In 1955 Tawney added a note that a distinguished journal of the time
'paid this article the compliment of describing it as "pert", and warned the editor
against publishing similar articles in future. For an article written over forty
years ago', added Tawney, 'this one, I think, is not bad.'—Ed.

70

often used today to suggest the same conclusion: that the single and all-sufficient test of the education which a group is to receive is the probable professional avocation of the majority of its members, provided that movement between different groups is sufficiently free to prevent the potential barrister or doctor being set to the bench. Society can be divided, it is thought, into those who work with their brains and those who work with their hands, and this division offers a decisive guide to educational policy. It is worth while to provide university education for the former. It is not worth while to provide it for the latter. 'A university,' said a distinguished professor in the presence of the writer, 'is simply the professional school of the brain-working classes.'

Now it would, of course, be folly to deny that there are large fields of education in which this statement has considerable truth. The majority of men—one may hope an increasing majority—must live by working. Their work must be of different kinds, and to do different kinds of work they need specialized kinds of professional preparation. Doctors, lawyers, engineers, plumbers and masons must, in fact, have trade schools of different kinds. The point at which this theory of the functions of the universities is challenged by the educational movement of labour is its doctrine that education which cannot, except by an unnatural distortion of terms, be called technical or professional, should be organized with a similar regard to the existing economic divisions of society, in particular its placid and impudent assumption, so popular with many educated people, that a 'humane education' is suitable for persons entering a certain restricted group of professions, to which attempts are now being made to add the direction of business, but that it is a matter with which the manual working classes have nothing to do.

Such a misinterpretation of the meaning of educational specialization is felt to be intellectually an imposture. If persons whose work is different require, as they do, different kinds of professional instruction, that is no reason why one should be excluded from the common heritage of civilization of which the other is made free by a university education, and from which, *ceteris paribus*, both, irrespective of their occupations, are equally capable, as human beings, of deriving spiritual sustenance. Those who have seen the inside both of lawyers' chambers and of coal mines will not suppose that of the inhabitants of these places of gloom the former are more constantly inspired by the humanities than are the latter, or that conveyancing is in itself a more liberal art than hewing.

The differentiation of humane education according to class is felt to be worse than a mere intellectual error on the part of those by whom such education has hitherto been managed. It is felt to be one of those blunders which reveal coarseness of spirit even more than confusion of mind. It is felt to be morally insulting. On the lips of many of its advocates it *is* morally insulting. Stripped of its decent draperies of convention, what it means is that there is a class of masters whose right it is to enter at manhood on the knowledge which is the inheritance of the race, and a class of servants whose hands should be taught to labour but whose eyes should be on the furrow which is watered with their sweat, whose virtue is contentment, and whose ignorance is the safety of the gay powers by whom their iron world is ruled. 'What,' said an educated man to the writer, 'you teach history and economics to miners and engineers? Take care. You will make them discontented and disloyal to us.' That division of mankind into those who are ends and those who are means, whether made by slaveholders or by capitalists, is the ultimate and unforgivable wrong, with which there can be truce neither in education nor in any other department of social life. To such wickedness only one answer is possible, *Ecrasez l'infame.*

But, it will be urged, secondary education is being improved. Rungs to connect it with the elementary schools at one end and with the universities at the other are being constructed. In time every clever child will have a chance of winning a scholarship and passing from the elementary school to the university. What more do you desire? Now, it need hardly be said, the creation of such increased facilities is a matter for congratulation, especially if it is accompanied by a provision for the scholarship winner sufficiently generous to overcome the heavy burden entailed upon his family by the loss of his earnings. How meagre these facilities are at the present time in proportion to the need for them, how illusory is the idea that more than a tiny fraction of the children qualified to make the best use of higher education receive it, what infinite misapplication of human capacity results from the fact that of the children leaving elementary schools less than five per cent pass each year to secondary schools, no one who has seen anything of working-class conditions of life needs to be told. It may truly be said that wisdom cries in the street and no man regards it, unless indeed it is so tired after ten hours in a mill that it cries at home. It is certainly not the case, however, that the only avenue to humane education of the highest kind ought to be that which consists in a career of continuous school attendance from five to eighteen.

In this matter we are still far too much at the mercy of the dogma of selection through competitive examinations which dominated the last half of the nineteenth century. Such selection has its use, and its use is to determine who are most suitable for a limited number of posts. But no one dreams of determining who shall enter elementary schools by a process of selection. On the contrary, we provide elementary education for all on the ground that it is indispensable to good citizenship. In the same way, side by side with the selective system created by means of scholarships, there ought to be a system of higher education which aims at, even though it cannot attain, universal provision, which is accessible to all who care to use it, and which is maintained not in order to enable intellect to climb from one position to another, but to enable all to develop the faculties which, because they are the attributes of man, are not the attributes of any particular class or profession of men. To suppose that the goal of educational effort is merely to convert into doctors, barristers, and professors a certain number of persons who would otherwise have been manual workers is scarcely less unintelligent than to take the Smilesian advice, 'Remember, my boy, that your aim should be to be master of that business', as an all-satisfying formula of economic progress, or to regard the existence of freedom as making tolerable the institution of slavery.

Selection is wanted to save us from incompetence in high places: if only one could add to the scholarship system by which capacity travels up, a system of negative scholarships which would help incapacity to travel down! Universal provision is wanted because society is one, because we cannot put our minds in commission, because no class is good enough to do its thinking for another. The ideas are not mutually exclusive: they are mutually complementary. It is not enough, for example, that some children should be removed from elementary schools, where classes are overcrowded and teachers overworked, to secondary schools where conditions are better. We want *all* the children to be given individual attention *in* the elementary schools. It is not enough that a few working-class boys and girls should be admitted to universities, and that many more will be admitted in the future. We want as much university education as we can get for the workers who *remain* workers all their lives.

The idea of social solidarity which is the contribution of the working classes to the social conscience of our age has its educational as well as its economic applications. What it implies is not merely *la carrière ouverte aux talents*, indispensable though that is, but *égalité de fait*, not simply equality of opportunity but universality of provision. Perhaps our educationalists have not hitherto allowed sufficiently for the surprising fact that there is no inconsiderable number of men and women whose incentive to education is not material success but spiritual energy, and who seek it, not in order that they may become something else, but because they are what they are. The oversight is not unnatural. The attitude is not one which is common in the ordinary seminaries of youth.

II. THE ORGANIZATION

The impulse which such ideas imperfectly express has come not from the authorities but from the rank and file, and, for that reason, it has been not simply an addition but an innovation. While the experts have been engaged in the necessary task of preparing machinery, the new spirit has been finding its way into higher education from those who have been hitherto better accustomed to see their educational destinies settled over their heads. Almost for the first time in English educational history the sedate rows of statistics which appear in Government Reports have suddenly begun to walk, to assert intellectual appetites, to demand that they shall be satisfied, to organize themselves in order to insist on their satisfaction—in short, to behave like men and women. The result, partially revealed in different ways by Ruskin College, by the Central Labour College, by the growth of innumerable classes and reading circles whose existence is almost unknown except to their members finds, perhaps, its completest expression in the Workers' Educational Association.

Not, of course, that the Association is labouring at an untilled field. Behind it lies a century of working-class educational effort. The high landmarks which stand out and are known to all, the educational work of the Co-operative movement, the rush to found Working Men's Colleges in the 1850s, the earlier years of University Extension in the north of England, rise from foundations laid by the faith of countless pioneers, humble men and women whose names are remembered lovingly in their own little towns and villages, who would have called themselves anything but educationalists, whose students were disciples rather than pupils, and whose influence an itinerant teacher can here and there trace today in the unexpected warmth of the welcome accorded him. Like all working-class movements, the Workers' Educational Association moves in a path worn smooth by the vanguard of the anonymous.

Founded in 1903 by a group of trade unionists and co-opera- tors, the Workers' Educational Association is a federation which at the present time includes a large number of working-class and educational organizations. Its organization has grown in the last few years with remarkable and rather disconcerting rapidity. Like trade unions, co-operative societies, and mediaeval gilds, the Workers' Educational Association is not limited by any articles of association to one specific purpose. Its aim is to articulate the educational aspirations of Labour, to represent them to the proper authorities, to stimulate into activity, when it exists, the organization through which they can be satisfied, to create it when it does not.

Necessarily, therefore, the work of the Association is in a constant state of transformation, and there are already signs of a widening in its horizon which is likely to cause it in the future to give increased attention to questions connected with the education of children and young persons. During the first ten years of its existence, however, its main task has been to create, with the assistance of the proper authorities, the nucleus of that system of humane education for adult workers, both men and women, which has attained some celebrity under the name of the University Tutorial Class movement.

The establishment of University Tutorial Classes is not by any means the only outcome of its labour. An energetic branch of the Association forms the centre of those educational activities of a district which, because they are not supported out of public money, do not fall within the province of the Local Education Authority, and offers a medium through which they are kept in communication with each other. The university spirit exists outside university cities, and such activities, at any rate in the north of England, are more numerous and more vigorous than might at first be supposed. A successful branch of the Workers' Educational Association secures the affiliation of all bodies carrying on any educational work, as well as of the local trade unions, trades councils, and co-operative societies which are its main support. With the assistance thus obtained it can take steps to meet the educational needs of different sections of the population in ways which vary according to the conditions of different localities, but which normally consist of the organization of lectures, classes, and reading circles. The strength of the movement is that by casting a wide net it is able to draw together all the educational forces of a district, to give the demand for higher education the support of a representative and democratic organization, and to build from within instead of borrowing from without. To build from within, to help men to develop their own genius, their own education, their own culture, that is the secret.

The first task, indeed, of any such society as the Workers' Educational Association is to lay to rest that smiling illusion which whispers that 'culture' is something that one class—'the educated'—possess, that another—'the uneducated'—are without, and that the former, when sufficiently warmed by sympathy or alarm, can transfer to the latter in pills made up for weak digestions. How venerably is this superstition rooted in the historical organization of English education! With what affection is it regarded by that not inconsiderable number of persons who possess sufficient money to be able to dispense with any other test of intellectual attainments! With what triumphant logic has the beautiful English arrangement by which wealth protects learning and learning in turn admits wealth as a kind of honorary member of its placid groves, enabled the upper classes to meet their inferiors! 'You see, my good friends, it is no use fighting against science. We govern you because we are wiser, because we have more knowledge, because we are *better educated* than you are!' The time appears to be coming when these inferiors do not listen so patiently as of old. 'Very well,' they say, 'granted for the sake of argument that you govern us because you are educated, and we are not educated because you have hitherto governed us, and made laws upon (among other matters) the subject of education, then we will have our own education. We will show what we can make of it, and what it will do for us.'

Of that answer the branches of the Workers' Educational Association are the first, not yet wholly self-confident, voice. Men meet and discuss. There is hesitation, curiosity, interest, eagerness for knowledge. We ought to have learned about that; can't we learn about it? We *will* learn about it, and we will find a man to help us if a man is to be found. Fortunate teacher, who is sought and not avoided! Thus the medium is created; the spirit finds a body; the solitary student discovers that he is one of a crowd. Education is not put on like varnish. It springs like a plant from the soil, and the fragrance of the earth is upon it.

Such work is at once educational and propagandist. It meets some of the needs of those who are beginning to demand higher education, and it creates a body of students who desire more advanced, systematic, and continuous study. The provision made for such students, or for some among them, consists of the University Tutorial Classes. A University Tutorial Class is really the nucleus of a university established in a place where no university exists. Its organization is simple. It consists of a group of not more than thirty students who agree to meet regularly once a week for twenty-four weeks during each of three successive winters for the purpose of study under a tutor appointed by a university, to follow the course of reading outlined by the tutor and to write fortnightly essays.

The classes meet every week for two hours at a time, of which the first normally consists of a lecture and the second of questions and discussion by the students. Books are obtained from the universities and from local libraries. The subjects of study are chosen by the classes themselves after consultation with the tutor. In the earlier years of the movement they consisted almost entirely of economic history and economics. But these subjects were interpreted in a very catholic sense, and included the consideration of a good many matters which would not, perhaps, figure largely in a university course on economics. At the present time the scope of the classes is tending to widen, and though economic history and economics still probably predominate, there are classes in literature, political science, general history, biology, psychology, and philosophy. And the classes *are* classes, not lectures. Thanks to the fact that they are small, tutor and students can meet as friends, discover each other's idiosyncrasies, and break down that unintentional system of mutual deception which seems inseparable from any education which relies principally on the formal lecture. It is often before the classes begin and after they end, in discussions round a student's fire, or in a walk to and from his home, that the root of the matter is reached both by student and tutor. The students themselves are drawn from almost every occupation, but the majority of them are manual workers.

If the University Tutorial Classes have shown that there is a wide demand for higher education of a humane type among the workers, it has shown also that there is a large number of workers who need only the opportunity to reach a very high level in their studies. It is as to the quality of the work done in the classes that the academic critic will naturally feel the greatest curiosity, and by which the movement will necessarily be judged by educationalists. The classes are fortunate in having from the first been closely watched by high academic authorities and by the inspectors of the Board of Education.

The disposition, which was occasionally shown in their earlier years, to regard them as an amiable, but quixotic, attempt to provide cheap culture 'for the masses', by populariz-ing subjects which lose their meaning when they lose their austerity, has, therefore, been brought from the beginning to the test of facts, and is no longer held by persons whose experi-ence or attainments entitle them to consideration. The verdict given in their report to the Board of Education by Professor L. T. Hobhouse and Mr Headlam, after an exhaustive examina-tion of a large number of classes, that their work was 'in some respects better, and in others not so good, as that of an Oxford or Cambridge undergraduate', that the classes 'tend to accustom the student to the ideal of work familiar at a university', and that 'as regards the standard reached, there are students whose essays compare favourably with the best academic work', is substantially that of most observers who have had experience of teaching in a university and who have seen the work of the Tutorial Classes at first hand.

Such a development means more than the addition of a few thousands to the ranks of university students. It means that we are approaching a period, such as existed sixty years ago, when it will be necessary to revise the meaning of the word university. The new interpretation of the meaning of a university education will be wider in two respects than that which has obtained hitherto. The conception of a university as the 'professional school of the brain-working classes' will not disappear, but it will be broadened to admit as genuine university students those who are not studying for the purpose of any profession except that of a reasonable and humane conduct of life. If the whole object of a university were to prepare those who enter it for specialized avocations, then it would indeed be the case that university education could never be enjoyed by men and women who depend on manual labour for their living, though it still might and should be far more accessible to their children than it is at present.

But is it? What is actually happening today is that the study under university teachers of the subjects taught in universities by the methods pursued in universities is being demanded and obtained by a growing number of men and women quite apart from the professional interests which it is one of the legitimate aims of a university to encourage. Since it will hardly be contended that a man obtains a university education when he studies history and philosophy in order to enter the Civil Service, and does not obtain it when he studies the same subject merely because he enjoys doing so, we must revise our conception of a university education so as to include in it all those, whatever their occupations, who are pursuing a regular course of university studies under the guidance of a university teacher.

And we must find room in our idea of university for students of mature years, who carry on their education in the midst of the routine of their working life. That education is never ended is one of those gracious commonplaces which mankind seems to have agreed to learn in its youth in order that it may disregard them when it reaches the age at which they become applicable. The conventional conception of education in England is of a continuous course of whole-time study from about the age of seven to that of twenty-one or twenty-two, and of university education as the final plunge in the bath of ideas before men 'turn from books to life'. This view of the place of university education, admirably adapted as it is to the needs of those from whom the demand for university education has hitherto principally come, need not be discarded. But it requires to be supplemented by a realization of the function which universities can fulfil in providing for the needs of those whose economic career is moulded on a different framework from that of the professional classes.

University Tutorial Classes are not, in short, an alternative to a university education, a *pis aller* for those who cannot 'go to a university'. Nor are they merely a preparation for study in a university. They are themselves a university education, carried on, it is true, under difficulties, but still carried on in such a way as to make their promotion one among the most important functions of a university. If this is not yet fully recognized it is because one of the besetting sins of those in high places in England—it is not that of the working classes—is the bad utilitarianism which thinks that the object of education is not education, but some external result, such as professional success or industrial leadership. It is not in this spirit that a nation can be led to believe in the value of the things of the mind. In the matters of the intellect, as in matters of religion, 'High Heaven rejects the lore of nicely calculated less or more'. And it is, perhaps, not fanciful to say that the disinterested desire of knowledge for its own sake, the belief in the free exercise of reason without regard to material results and because reason is divine, a faith not yet characteristic of English life, but which it is the highest spiritual end of universities to develop, finds in the Tutorial Classes of the Workers' Educational Association as complete an expression as it does within the walls of some university cities. To these miners and weavers and engineers who pursue knowledge with the passion born of difficulties, knowledge can never be a means, but only an end; for what have they to gain from it save knowledge itself?

Historians tell us that decadent societies have been revivified through the irruption of new races. In England a new race of nearly 900,000 souls bursts upon us every year. They stand on the threshold with the world at their feet, like barbarians gazing upon the time-worn plains of an ancient civilization. If, instead of rejuvenating the world, they grind corn for the Philistines and doff bobbins for mill-owners, the responsibility is ours into whose hands the prodigality of Nature pours life itself, and who let it slip aimlessly through the fingers that close so greedily on material riches.

7

THE WORKERS' EDUCATIONAL
ASSOCIATION AND ADULT EDUCATION[1]

I am not myself a passionate devotee of ceremonial occasions. They are apt to be accompanied by orgies of self-applause, of a kind to provoke the judgment of Heaven. It is proper, nevertheless, that we should fortify ourselves for future tasks by surveying the ground already travelled, should compare achievements with hopes, and should ponder the lessons both of opportunities missed and of successes won. If I were asked where I received the best part of my own education, I should reply, not at school or college, but in the days when as a young, inexperienced and conceited teacher of Tutorial Classes, I underwent, week by week, a series of friendly, but effective, deflations at the hands of the students composing them. The Association was not in those distant days the power which it has since become. Sections of opinion divided in everything were united in regarding it with flattering alarm. Left-wing movements were suspicious. If a minority of universities were cordial, not a few were sceptical or indifferent. Local Education Authorities, to whom during the last quarter of a century we have owed so deep a debt, had at that time other fish to fry, and, with some notable exceptions, did not always receive us with open arms.

On the contrast between the conditions of that age of sanguine irresponsibility and those of today I need not dwell at length. It is sufficient to recall that the handful of pioneers has become a national organization, with a thousand-odd branches grouped in twenty-one Districts, and a student membership of

[1] A lecture delivered on 8 May, 1953, at the invitation of the Council for Extra-Mural Studies of the University of London on the occasion of the Fiftieth Anniversary of the Workers' Education Association. Published by the University of London, Athlone Press, 1953.

over a hundred thousand; that the contacts of the Association with organized labour have grown closer year by year; that it no longer has to explain the reasons for its existence to universities and L.E.A.s, but co-operates with the great majority of both on easy and cordial terms; and, most significant, perhaps, of all, that the cause for which it stands has won a measure of public recognition not formerly accorded it.

A precipitate enthusiasm for audacious novelties is not among the characteristic weaknesses of our fellow-countrymen. It has taken half a century to convince them that educational work of the kind on which we are engaged is not a mere innocuous superfluity, but a vital element in the life of a self-respecting democracy. As was shown by the recent proposal—now temporarily, it appears, withdrawn—to save something under £40,000 a year at the cost of closing some hundreds of our classes, the conversion is, unfortunately, still far from complete. If, however, it is under way, the Association, though not it alone, may fairly claim some part in the process of enlightment.

All this is a matter for legitimate self-congratulation. But movements, like individuals, should beware when all men speak well of them. Neglect and unpopularity are bad, but respectability and complacency are worse; and, when a cause has achieved a modest measure of success, its adherents should redouble their vigilance to ensure that it is not merely floating with the current, but inspired by specific and distinctive aims, to which it is faithful in rough weather as well as calm, and judges its activities by the degree to which they promote the attainment of them.

Books on education, with some exceptions, belong to a type of literature which, I am sorry to say, I cannot read, and to inflict on you a discourse on that subject is beyond my power. Stripped of technicalities, the essence of the matter, so far as it concerns us, seems to me pretty simple. Everyone, whether he intends it or not, adopts some attitude to the world of human beings in which his lot is cast; and, as that attitude is, so in large measure will be both his personal happiness and his utility to his fellows. It may be one of sympathy and co-operation, or of antagonism and suspicion. Education, as I see it, though it is much else as well, is partly, at least, the process by which we transcend the barriers of our isolated personalities, and become partners in a universe of interests which we share with our fellow-men, living and dead alike. No one can be fully at home in the world unless, through some acquaintance with literature and art, the history of society and the revelations of science, he has seen enough of the triumphs and tragedies of mankind to realize the heights to which human nature can rise and the depths to which it can sink.

It is partly, of course, a question of knowledge, but not of knowledge alone. It is possible to be learned and a fool; universities are not without—but that is a reflection which, in the presence of the Vice-Chancellor, I must not pursue. It is still more a question of imagination, of reflection, of the mental initiative and independence which sees through conventional shams to realities, and of the confidence which only independence of spirit can give. The purpose of an adult education worthy of the name is not merely to impart reliable information, important though that is. It is still more to foster the intellectual vitality to master and use it, so that knowledge becomes, not a burden to be borne or a possession to be prized, but a stimulus to constructive thought and an inspiration to action.

All serious educational movements have in England been also social movements. They have been the expression in one sphere—the training of mind and character—of some distinctive conception of the life proper to man and of the kind of society in which he can best live it. Our Association is no exception. It was born in the social ferment of the opening decade of the present century, when, with the passage of the Acts of 1902 and 1903, public education had just started on the second stage of its great career, and the world of Labour was heaving with the long ground-swell which found its political expression in 1906, and its industrial in the Trade Union upheaval of 1910–13. Mansbridge,[1] whose genius discerned and voiced the unformulated educational aspirations, which were another aspect of the same popular agitation, owed much both to the long educational tradition of the Co-operative Movement, which, as an employee of the Co-operative Wholesale Society, he served, and to the influence of the University Extension Lectures. He felt, however, that both had, for the

[1] Albert Mansbridge was Founder and first General Secretary of the WEA.—Ed.

time being, shot their bolts, and that, if anything serious in the sphere of education for adult workers was to be achieved, a new start must be made.

His dominant conceptions were three. The first inspired his unwearying assertion that the mass of ordinary men and women, who did not, in the elegant language of the day, 'climb the educational ladder', needed a humane education as much, and could turn it to as good account, as the minority who succeeded in those athletic feats. The second consisted in his reiterated conviction that the proper vehicle of such education was to be found, not primarily in lectures, valuable though they often were, to large and miscellaneous audiences, but in a group or class sufficiently small for intimate relations to develop between its members and between them and the tutor, and sufficiently continuous to exercise a genuine influence on all attending it. The third was his insistence that workers' education could become a power only if based, not on plans, however well-intentioned, devised from above by academic institutions and public authorities, but on an equal partnership between the bodies providing facilities and an organization commanding the confidence and voicing the views of the actual and potential students whom the Association founded by him exists to serve.

It was in the application of these principles that the Mansbridgian revolution consisted. It was they which gave its character to the WEA, the Tutorial Class movement, and all subsequent developments, such as the Summer Schools, derived from the same source. The aim of the Association, therefore, was not merely to multiply classes, though naturally it welcomed their growth, but to create an organization through those who in the past, if they remained in contact with education after leaving school, had too often been passive recipients of the variety offered them; they should formulate their own views of the type of education desired by them and determine the lines on which it should proceed. It judged the success of its classes, not only by the progress of their members' studies, but also by the degree to which the knowledge gained and habits formed aided fruitful activities in the affairs of daily life. It sought, in addition to making individual students, to awaken working-class movements as a whole to a keener consciousness both that the promotion of adult education among their younger members and—not less essential—the improvement of public education are of vital importance to the cause for which such movements stand. It regarded education, in short, neither primarily as a hobby or pastime—both excellent things—nor as an avenue to individual self-advancement, but as a social dynamic. In the words of the Statement of Policy appended to our Constitution, it valued adult education 'not only as a means of developing individual character and capacity, but as a preparation for the exercise of social rights and responsibilities'.

The reasons which lead men and women of mature years to devote part of their leisure to study are, inevitably and properly, of great diversity. Our business, in my view, is not to prescribe the lines which different individuals and groups should pursue, but to do our best, within our own field of non-vocational education, to meet their varying requirements, whatever these may be. In the distant days when I was a tutor, the prevalent demand was for Economic History and Theory, of the former of which I learned something at the expense of my unhappy students, while the latter—a not less valuable lesson—I quickly discovered to be out of my depth. Today a third, or more, of our students are in classes engaged in the study of literature, music, painting or one or other of the other arts. Such subjects are concerned, not merely with the machinery of existence, but with the things which make it worth while to live. We ought warmly to welcome the tendencies revealed by the growing demand for them.

Actually, of course, different interests are not mutually exclusive. The most brilliant of recent economists, the late Lord Keynes, was a knowledgeable critic of pictures. To pore over the details of Jacobean economic life, while ignoring the drama of the age is absurd. Nor will a man make much of the social history of the nineteenth century, unless he adds to the study of blue-books and other dull works an acquaintance with its novels. Nevertheless, it is natural and not improper that social studies in a more specific sense—History, Economics, International Affairs, Political Science, Sociology, and other subjects concerned with the life of man in society—should continue to be chosen by more than half our classes. One of the features of recent academic progress has been the expansion of such studies in the universities. It would be surprising if adult classes, composed of men and women confronted daily by the problems with which the subjects in question deal, had gone a different way.

It would also, I think, be unfortunate. I recall an eminent French historian, the late Professor Halévy, remarking, a decade before events gave a fresh confirmation to his words, that all the great crises of European history had been at the same time both wars and revolutions. If the last term be interpreted, as it should be, to cover any comprehensive reconstruction of institutions, irrespective of the methods employed to effect it, then Europe is experiencing today the results of both. It is wrestling, as best it may, with the legacy of the first. It is passing, in certain not unimportant regions, through the opening phases of the second. In such circumstances, the sensation of bewilderment, to which, I suppose, most candid persons, on contemplating the world about them, would confess, is not surprising. An immense effort of adaptation is needed to adjust old ideas to new realities. Carrying, as we do, the assumptions, prejudices, psychological and social resistance mechanisms appropriate to one kind of world into the novel environment of another, we often find that effort beyond our power.

Examples are endless, and I confine myself to a handful. We live in a civilization combining economic interdependence with political diversity. Neither feature is so new as is sometimes supposed; but it is only too clear that the mixture can, under modern conditions, be explosive. An immense amount of thought has been devoted since the war to the search for formulae of salvation, from world government to some modest form of regional federation or functional co-operation. What should laymen like ourselves think about the remedies proposed? How, again, do we visualize the economic future of this country in the circumstances in which, while remaining, as I think, a political and cultural leader, it is materially a power of the second class? Is the right reaction to the present unbalance of the world economy to be found, as at present seems to be thought, in the struggle for a larger hold on the American market? Or in a closer partnership with the Continent and the Dominions? Or in a more intensive development of internal resources? Or in all three at once?

A shift—to turn to matters nearer home—in the internal balance of economic power is clearly under way. It will, of course, undergo the usual recurrent oscillations and temporary arrests; but it is unlikely, in my judgment, to be reversed. Given the assumption that the aim of social policy should be to ensure that the conditions of a good life are shared as equally as is possible by all, how do past proposals for attaining that end look today, and in what respects, if any, do they require to be revised or supplemented? During the last fifteen years or so Trade Unionism seems to have entered on a new phase in its career. Its dual character as a body of professional associations and an organ of agitation has been maintained and strengthened, but, half-unconsciously, it has added to those familiar roles a third. In fact, if not yet in theory, it has come increasingly to exercise a measure of responsibility, not merely for the protection of its members in matters of wages, hours and working conditions, but for more general issues of economic strategy. That is obviously so on the upper levels of the industries—now roughly, in terms of workers employed, one-fifth of the industrial sector—in public ownership, though not yet, it seems, in individual pits or plants. The situation in private undertakings is different; but here also the pressure of the workers in them for a voice in their control is likely to increase. What precisely do such demands involve? What obligations will they, if successful, entail? How best can trade unions equip themselves and their members for the enlarged responsibilities and powers rightly, in my opinion, claimed by them?

Experience suggests that, in order to induce the British public to undertake educational reconstruction, nothing less than a major war will suffice. Unfortunately these expensive curtain-raisers produce a double result. They facilitate legislation, much of which, no doubt, had on the last occasion been long prepared, but which only the explosion made it possible to enact. They create a situation in which the legislation, when passed, is difficult to apply. What steps should be taken to ensure that the principles of the Act of 1944, much of which is at present in cold storage, shall become a practical reality?

I do not pretend to possess an answer to these conundrums or to the numberless other questions which arise in one's mind;

but obviously they are important, and each includes a host of secondary problems. Reduced to essentials, politics, it may be suggested, is, or ought to be, the art of achieving by collective action ends which cannot be attained with the same measure of success by individual effort, and often cannot be attained by it at all. The master of politics, as of other arts, does not come by nature. It has to be acquired. It is acquired partly by practice, but partly also by study and reflection, without which practice will not yield its lessons. We may, of course, prefer to live in a state of innocence, untroubled by such issues. We can, if we please, resign the search for solutions of our problems to the superior wisdom of persons who are delighted, if we will let them, to do our thinking for us. We can, again, evade the perplexities which that search involves by taking refuge in the illusory consolations of dogmatic ideologies, whose votaries, by claiming the possession of prefabricated formulae adequate to all situations, are dispensed from the necessity of grappling seriously with any one of them.

But, if we reject both these primrose paths to futility—if we intend to use our eyes, and clear our minds of cant, and see the world as it is—only one alternative remains. It is that we should resolve, for two or three hours out of the hundred or so of our waking week, to consider these matters of permanent and general significance with somewhat the same seriousness that we bring to our private affairs; to do what we can to ascertain essential facts; and, since none of us can hope to travel far towards truth alone, to seize every opportunity to correct our limitations and enlarge our horizons by co-operative study and discussion with our fellows.

It is such opportunities, among others, which the Association exists to provide. It is sometimes suggested that the objective study of subjects such as some of those to which I have referred is rendered impossible by the political emotions associated with them. I do not share that view. All of them are regularly studied in universities, on the whole with beneficial results. There is no reason to suppose that disciplines providing a wholesome nutriment within those institutions are transformed into poisons outside them. Personally, as a teacher of Tutorial Classes, I never felt tempted to engage in propaganda. A doubtless very improper conceit persuaded me that the world, when enlightened, would agree with me. I thought, therefore, that the longest way round was the shortest way home, and that my job was to promote enlightenment. Nor, I should add, did my students expect or desire propaganda from me. They had no high opinion of my oratorical powers, and were well aware that they needed only to lift a finger to obtain any Sunday in the month a more effective propagandist than myself. In reality, of course, the way for an institution or movement to achieve impartiality is not to attempt to chase all the partialities out; for, being human, we can none of us be other than partial. It is to draw as many as possible of the partialities in, on two conditions. The first is that, if the spirit moves their votaries to propagate a creed, they shall do so by the frank exchange of open argument, not by subterranean intrigues. The second is that they shall accord to the opinions of their neighbours, however nauseating or absurd, the same respectful hearing which they claim for their own.

Tolerance and the appeal to reason have been on the whole, I think, the spirit of the WEA. The Association obviously works today in conditions widely different from those of its youth. I refer, not merely to the profounder knowledge and more scintillating intelligence of the present generation, but to the greatly expanded facilities—an expansion which we warmly welcome—supplied by agencies other than ourselves. Section 42 of the Act of 1944, which imposed on Local Education Authorities the obligation to make provision, after consultation with universities and Educational Associations, for the education of adults, opened a new era. The resources of Education Authorities enable them to function on a scale which no voluntary organization can attempt to rival. We should regard with cordial satisfaction the growth of this branch of their work. When they take, as the great majority of them do, a reasonably catholic view of their responsibilities, I see no ground at all for supposing that their heightened activity in the sphere of adult education will be other than beneficial, not only to the country as a whole, but to the voluntary bodies concerned, and, in particular, to the WEA. In education, 'to divide is not to take away'. The larger the supply, and the wider the interest aroused, the more general the demand. Provided that our Association lives up to its pretensions, the number of those who find in its classes, with their combination of intellectual keenness, social idealism and comradeship, something which specially appeals to them, will always be more than sufficient to tax our resources to the full.

Our relations with the majority of academic institutions have long been so cordial that I need not dwell on them. The universities have done much for the WEA. We, in our modest way, have, I think, done something for them. It has been, in my view, beneficial to the academic departments concerned with history, economics, political science and other studies concerned with the life of society that so many of their younger members should have experienced the combined stimulus and discipline of intimate contact with men and women of mature years, with an outlook on life and approach to those subjects different from their own. I can never be sufficiently grateful for the lessons learned from the adult students whom I was supposed to teach, but who, in fact, taught me, and I know that many tutors in our Movement would say the same. Nor is it a small thing that one important and growing branch of academic work should be supervised by committees representing universities, Local Education Authorities and working-class bodies. Any doctrinaire can draw the blue-prints for a simpler and more symmetrical design; but that co-operative organization, with the interplay of varying interest and attitudes facilitated by it, has possessed one capital advantage which a neat division of functions would not, to the same degree, have secured. It has helped to build a bridge of mutual understanding between academic institutions, public educational administration and popular movements, which has been of benefit, not only to all of them, but to the nation as a whole. In no other European country known to me could a similar partnership in adult education exist. Its success in our own should be regarded with pride.

But, of course, grateful though we are to our allies, the universities, the Local Education Authorities, and, not least, the officials of the Ministry, it is on the outlook and aspirations of its members that the future of the Association depends. A society requires for its health both tenacity in adhering to its distinctive aims and flexibility in the choice of methods to attain them. Those engaged in the day-to-day work of administration are apt to lay most emphasis on the second quality;

but, on a longer view, the most important is the first. There are periods in the history of most organizations when they are tempted to follow the line of least resistance; and the line of least resistance is, in my experience, almost always wrong. The pursuit of it may produce imposing statistical results; but in education it is quality—by which I mean, not cleverness, but seriousness, judgment and conviction—that counts for most. Our objectives are, as they always have been, simplicity itself. The Association, in the first place, is not a universal provider. Not only does it lack the means for so ambitious a role, but, as the title chosen for it by its founder shows, such is not its function. We interpret the word 'workers' in no narrow sense; but our primary mission, proclaimed from hundreds of platforms and in scores of pamphlets, is to the educationally under-privileged majority, who cease their full-time education at or about fifteen, and who need a humane education both for their personal happiness and to help them to mould the society in which they live. Our duty to them is equally obvious. It is not to delude them with the mendacious pretence that an education worth having is a less exacting alternative to the cinema, dogs, darts or the austerities of the daily Press. It is to put them on their mettle, to pitch our claims high, and to rely for a response to them, not on the insignificance of the effort which they demand, but on the magnitude of the reward which effort will bring, in the discovery of powers previously unrealized and enlarged capacities for effective action. I am told that such a policy will diminish the number of our classes. It may, for the time being; but the prospect of a temporary decline does not dismay me. The genuineness, rather than the mere bulk, of its work has been the Association's longest suit. It will dilute that virtue at its peril.

It is of the nature of a democratic society that the task of keeping it true to the educational and social ideals with which it started on its career should be the responsibility, not primarily of its officers, but of the membership as a whole. If it be asked how the Association has grown, the answer must be, I think, less by organized propaganda, though that has played its part, than through the influence of individuals conscious of the benefits which they have derived from its work and anxious that their friends and fellow-workers should share them. The field for missionary enterprise of that kind remains immense. The appreciation of the importance of education is far stronger and more widespread that it was in the early days of the WEA, but a push is still often needed to convert sympathy into action. It is for the rank and file of our Movement to ensure that the stimulus is supplied. They can be vigilant in pressing for improvements in public education; can help to draw trade unions and co-operative societies into affiliation with the WEA, and, by making more widely known the opportunities offered not only by our classes, but by the weekend and summer schools of the WETUC, can do much to create the alert and well-informed membership which those movements need. Such work is laborious, but its fruits are worth the effort. I do not doubt that, as in the past, our members and students will rise to the height of the occasion.

PART III
POLITICS

8

THE CONDITIONS OF ECONOMIC LIBERTY[1]

Whatever may be the military and diplomatic issue of the present conflict, one prediction may be made with confidence. It is that the social and political existence of the majority of Englishmen now living will be dominated by the forces which the war has released. Russia may be the only country to depose its old *régime* amid the rattle of machine-guns, because Russia was the only country where the political system was too brittle to change and too odious to endure. But the significance of moral and economic forces is not limited to the varying national forms in which they find expression. If Russia is the only country where the war has meant an explosion, there is no country in which it has not closed an epoch; and the parliaments of England and France will be as powerless to revive the past as the Romanoffs were to maintain it. Nor, indeed, does it seem probable that the public will desire them to do so. It speaks of reconstruction. But by reconstruction it means not the resuscitation of the past, but reform. This is a war after which there will be no Restoration.

The England of 1920 will differ from that of 1914, not merely because it has passed through a new Industrial Revolution, but because of a new quality in its moral and intellectual atmosphere. Partly as the culmination of movements at work in all European countries before 1914, partly as the result of the development of thought in the forcing-house of war, the world has been prepared, side by side with the practical innovations in its industrial organization, for a revolution in the standards by which industry and social life are judged. Not merely the facts, but the minds which appraise them, have been profoundly modified, and the mere material readjust-

[1] Chapter in *Labour and Capital after the War*, a symposium by various writers. Edited by S. J. Chapman. John Murray, London, 1918.

ments in the technique of industry, which supply the text to discussions of reconstruction in the Press and on the platform, will in a few years, it may be anticipated, prove the least of the changes induced by the war.

When peace returns, it will not be sufficient, therefore, merely to accept and legitimize the *fait accompli*. It will not be enough simply to acquiesce in those industrial changes which have been proved by experience to contribute to economic efficiency, and to introduce only such reforms as may be needed to regularize the situation, to smooth the transition to normal industry, or to buttress the weak spots in economic organization which the war may have revealed. The publicists and politicians who think that the situation can be met by speeding up the economic machine, and by giving all classes some share in the increased output, while leaving their relative position and status unaltered, are building castles on land already cut off by the sea. Whatever may be the merits of particular items in these programmes of national strength and industrial productivity, the programmes, as a whole, are tragically irrelevant. They are conceived on the wrong plane. They are anachronisms.

They are conceived on the wrong plane, because they omit the two vital elements in the situation. The first is the demand for radical social reconstruction, which was gathering weight long before the war made reconstruction an official policy. The second is the impetus to that demand given by the participation of almost the whole young manhood of Europe in a war during which an immense debate upon political principles has been tossed from corner to corner of Europe and America, over the heads of the combatants in the trenches. The war has not created the problems which reform must solve; it has only been the lightning which revealed them. When the nation found its soldiers and sailors threatened with a shortage of munitions and coal, because employers and employees could not agree as to the terms upon which their industries should be carried on, it was merely reaping in three years the harvest of seed sown for three generations. It was not overwhelmed by an unprecedented emergency. It was found out by its old sins. The question is not how to repair an industrial system dislocated by war. It is how to reform an industrial system which was felt to be incompatible with social freedom and justice in peace. We have to revise the work not of four years but of a century and a half. The quarrel is not merely with the catastrophic changes of 1914 to 1919, but with the economic order of the age which began with the spinning-jenny and ended with the great war—of 1760 to 1914. Social Reconstruction either means Social Revolution, or it means nothing.

The problem is not new, and the principles by which it must be solved are not new. They are those which have been the daily bread of millions of men and women during the present tragedy, which have inspired the living, have comforted the bereaved, and have been hallowed by the dead. War is always shocking; but its remoter influence upon domestic policy and social organization depends, to no small extent, upon the motives to which it has appealed for support. If domestic reaction was the natural consequence of the arrogant nationalism which was the note of Germany in 1870, and of England in 1793, it is not too sanguine to believe that the liberal and humane ideals which, whatever may be true of governments, have been a spell to bind the common people of England and France to a hateful duty, will be a potent force for internal reform when they lay down their arms. Political thought and emotion cannot be penned in compartments. Right as the basis of human association, freedom for weak as strong, the moral law in public affairs—such ideas have a reference to social organization as well as to international policy.

Men who have read President Wilson's speeches in the intervals of a bombardment, or reflected upon Belgium before they went over the top, will be a little incredulous when they are told that the application of these principles to economic life and industrial organization would involve readjustments too disturbing to be tolerated. When they can measure the full effect of the new industrial revolution, their incredulity will become vocal. They were told by philosophers and politicians that social change, if practicable, could only be gradual. Now they will discover that the economic mechanism, which seemed so ponderous and rigid, has been transformed in three years by a collective act of will, because there was a strong enough motive, which was not an economic motive, to transform it.

They were told that the nation was too poor to offer the material conditions of a life of health and economic freedom to all its citizens. They will return to find it spending in a month more than the whole sum which it used to spend on education, public health, and housing in the course of a year, and in four months a sum equal to the total wage-bill of the country before the war. Unless the air of England is surprisingly different from that of France, they will ask whether this revelation of the possibilities of social transformation and of national resources does not contain lessons capable of application in time of peace.

Such issues will confront all nations; but they should appeal, above all, to Englishmen. They should appeal to them because England was the power which led Europe into the labyrinth of modern industrialism, and the greatest contribution which it can make to human progress is to guide the world towards economic reconstruction, as two hundred and fifty years ago it guided it towards constitutional government.

An industry, when all is said, is something in its essence quite simple. It is nothing more mysterious than a body of men associated, in various degrees of competition and co-operation, to win their living by providing the community with some service which it requires. Organize it as you will, let it be a group of craftsmen labouring with hammer and chisel, or peasants ploughing their own fields, or armies of mechanics of a hundred different trades constructing ships which are miracles of complexity with machines which are the climax of centuries of science and invention, its function is service, its method is association.

Because service is its function, an industry as a whole has rights and duties towards the community, the abrogation of which involves privilege. Because its method is association, the different parties within it have rights and duties towards each other, and their neglect or perversion involves oppression. Now the subordination of strength and intelligence to the public service, and the organization of civil association in accordance with justice and freedom, are tasks in which the larger England of history may not unreasonably claim to have achieved such success as falls to the lot of political humanity. Let her recognize the industrial problem for what it is, and she will solve it by her ancient methods worked out in her ancient spirit.

But she must recognize the nature of the problem. If the political genius of Englishmen is to be brought to bear upon industrial issues, industrial issues must be understood for what they are. They must cease to be sophisticated by being treated as exclusively or predominantly an economic issue, to be discussed in economic terms, and to be solved by economic considerations. Economic efficiency is one element, but only one, and not the most important element, in questions which, so far as they are concerned with the individual, are human or spiritual, and, in so far as they are concerned with society, are political, in the larger sense of the word 'politics'. There has been no more mischievous habit of thought than the smiling illusion which erected into a philosophy the conception that industry is a mechanism, moving by quasi-mechanical laws and adjusted by the play of non-moral forces, in which methods of organization and social relationships are to be determined solely by considerations of economic convenience and productive efficiency. By erecting an artificial barrier between the economic life of society and its religion, its art, the moral traditions and kindly feelings of human beings, that doctrine degrades the former and sterilizes the latter.

Englishmen must repudiate an inhuman philosophy of economic life for the same reason as they resist an unmoral philosophy of politics. Superficially attractive by reason of the short cut which it seems to offer to material success, that glittering creed involves the subordination of all the finer elements in the human spirit to the worship of power. The intellect of England swallowed it for three generations. But then its intellect is not England's strong point. The popular instinct of the nation, not to mention the conscience of its prophets and the imagination of its poets, has always abhorred it. The perpetual *malaise* which its application to industry has caused in the body politic shows that it is uncongenial to our deeper selves.

Since an industry, and the different parts of it, is at bottom merely one kind of association, it is inevitable that those concerned in it should apply to it their political traditions, and judge it by its conformity with them. Of those political traditions the most powerful is that group of ideas which are summarized by the word 'freedom'. The idea of economic freedom offers a fascinating and neglected theme to the philosophical historian, and is the greatest single force in the social agitations of the present day. In countries where ideas are disentangled from their application, it is a banner under which men march. In England, where remedies are stated and principles implied, the demand for economic liberty takes the form of an attack upon individual and concrete economic grievances.

These grievances are often summarized as poverty. But the summary is misleading. In so far as poverty arises from the niggardliness of nature or the natural defects of human character, it is an evil, but it is not a grievance. What gives it its sting, what converts economic misery into a political issue or a moral problem, is the conviction that the poverty of the modern world, since it is co-existent with riches, is unlike the natural poverty of the colonist, the fisherman, or the peasant, in being a social institution. Tyranny is none the less tyranny because it is unconscious, well-meaning, or even independent of the individual volition of those by whom it is exercised. Social poverty is merely one outward expression, impressive because it appeals to the eye, of the power over the lives of mankind which modern industrialism confers upon those who direct industry and control the material equipment upon which both industry and social life depend. The fundamental grievance is not a mere deficency of material resources. Hunger and cold cause misery, but men do not revolt against winter or agitate against the desert. The fundamental grievance is that the government of industry and the utilization both of capital and land are autocratic. From men's exclusion from control over the organization and apparatus of industry flow the particular grievances which are the spur to their discontent. Their ability to add synthesis to analysis, and to see their evils in their causes, not merely in their effects, is the measure of their intelligence.

It is no answer to the demand for economic freedom to point out that flesh is heir to evils which no social change can remedy. For the significance of liberty is that it supplies a touchstone by which men can discriminate between misery which is avoidable and misery which is not. It enables them to prevent that which can be prevented. Apart from the material evils which irresponsible power produces, it is alien to the political traditions of Englishmen that the livelihood of many should be dependent upon the arbitrary decision of a few, or that they should be governed in their daily lives by regulations in the making of which they have had no voice.

Stated in its most general form, therefore, the first problem of industrial organization is to create in every industry which is not a matter of individual handicraft or shop-keeping a constitution securing its members an effective voice in its government. The conditions of economic liberty require, in fact, like the conditions of religious liberty, to be restated. For the last two centuries economic freedom has been interpreted to mean the right of each individual to be unfettered by authority in pursuing whatever occupation he pleases in the way which he may think best, just as religious freedom has meant merely absence of interference with the right of the individual to believe and worship as he may choose.

This negative conception of liberty requires to be set in its place as one element in a more positive and constructive interpretation. Freedom, to be complete, must carry with it not merely the absence of repression but also the opportunity of self-organization. It must confer the right to associate with others in building up a social organization with a consciousness and corporate life of its own. Economic freedom must develop, in short, through the applications of representative institutions to industry. Except in the backwaters untouched, for good or evil, by the spirit of modern industrialism, it must rest on the recognition that all grades of workers in an industry and in every unit of it, from the organizer to the labourer, constitute a real community, and that in that community industrial sovereignty, subject (inevitable contradiction) to the larger sovereignty of the community, resides. Their freedom is simply their corporate power to control the conditions upon which their livelihood depends.

Their freedom must be corporate, because economic forces have decided that in all the staple industries production shall be corporate. In the shipbuilding industry, in transport, in the production of iron and steel, in the textile trades, in building, in general engineering, the firm which is the unit of the industry may include anything from a few hundred to several thousand workmen. It is a little society which is more populous than any village, sometimes more populous than many famous cities of the past. But, except for the Factory Acts and for the limited power of trade unionism, it is a society without a constitution and without a charter securing the rights of its members.

Consider the position of a worker in such a firm. Politically a citizen, in industry he is neither a citizen nor a partner, but a hand. He is taken on when there is work; he is dismissed when there is not. If the trade is 'organized' he may, through his Union, have a more or less effective voice in the settlement of wages and hours. If it is unorganized, the wages will tend to be the minimum needed to secure, under the pressure of competition, his services, and the hours the maximum which suit the convenience of the firm. As to the larger question of industrial policy, even as to details of workshop administration which vitally affects him, he has often no voice at all. In many industries methods of payment which he detests, like the premium bonus system, may be imposed upon him in spite of his protests. Piece rates may be arranged and rearranged without his being consulted and on no principle which he can understand, except that they will be reduced if he earns more than is thought to be 'enough for a workman'. He may have his livelihood abolished without compensation by the introduction of a new process or of machinery. He may suggest an improve- which would increase output, and either be snubbed for his pains or receive no adequate payment for it. He may be dismissed without appeal because he asks awkward questions, and he may, when dismissed, be prevented from getting employment in another shop by being blacklisted as an 'agitator'. Employment may be casual, as at most docks, because those who control it find it would be less convenient or more expensive to employ a regular staff, and as a result a whole district may be demoralized.

The smaller the town—and it must be remembered that there are still many towns which are almost dependent on less than half a dozen great firms—the more obvious and absolute the influence upon the social life of the local employers. If one large business is badly managed, or goes on short time for eighteen months while paying at the same time (as in an instance in the writer's experience) a dividend of twenty per cent, a whole district may be temporarily half-starved, without possessing even the right to protest. What is this except 'to live at the will of a lord'?

The alternative to industrial autocracy must be found in the development of associations through which the mass of the workers, in each industry as a whole, and in the units which compose it, can take part in its policy and organization through representatives whom they choose . . . The starting-point for such a development must obviously be trade unionism. A beginning would be made if the principle of trade unionism were applied not merely, as at present, to questions of wages and hours, but to all questions of industrial policy and workshop organization. Such a change involves a readjustment of the fluctuating boundary which at present separates 'labour' from 'management'. The readjustment will often be difficult, but it is imperative. It is imperative not because management is unimportant, but because its importance is so crucial that it is vital that it should have behind it the confidence of all who are affected by it.

'What touches all should be approved by all.' It need not be denied that an authority which is irresponsible is nevertheless often humane and far-sighted. But the claim of the employer, as it is sometimes interpreted, to 'manage his business as he pleases', not only involves in effect a demand that he should be free to impose upon men conditions of work against their will, but can also be used to undermine the control by trade unionism over wages and hours of labour in which most employers have at length, after a century of struggle, acquiesced. If a firm can introduce into the organization of its works what changes it will, if it can alter piece rates as it pleases without having to justify the alteration to those affected by it, if it can rearrange processes and introduce new machinery without the workers being consulted, if it can dismiss whom it chooses without being obliged to give any account of its decision, it can, in effect, stultify trade unionism, even while according it a nominal recognition.

Thus interpreted, freedom of management carries with it a control over the worker which is incompatible with civil liberty. It is incompatible, also, with economic efficiency. Indeed, the greatest single obstacle to the efficiency of industry is precisely the industrial autocracy which is supposed today to be the condition of attaining it, as two hundred and fifty years ago men looked to absolutism as the crown of statecraft, and wondered at the tumultuous disorderliness of Englishmen. If men are treated as 'hands', if they are told that 'the best workman is the man who obeys orders and doesn't pretend to think', they may give their hands, but they will withhold their brains. The only guarantee of efficient work, whether on the part of a company in the trenches or of men in a workshop, is not the 'discipline' of fear, but goodwill and mutual confidence.

If mutual confidence is to be the basis of industry, the organization of industry must be such as to deserve it. It must be based on some kind of constitution. Precisely what form an industrial constitution should take is a question which will be answered differently in different industries. Nor will any one answer be final. The policy which has recently been popularized, as offering at least the basis of it, is the creation in the staple industries of permanent National Councils of employers and workers, together with the establishment of district and workshop committees in different districts and in individual workshops. Were this proposal carried out, the function of the National Councils would be, not merely to deal with disagreements, but to consider the general policy and needs of each industry as a whole, to represent them to the public, and to recommend to, or even to impose upon recalcitrant minorities a line of action in accordance with them.

The establishment of workshop committees would involve a surrender by employers of their claim to freedom of management, and would mean that questions of workshop discipline and organization were settled in consultation with the workers in each shop. It would be for the National Councils, in the first place, to define the matters to be submitted to them. But among such matters would obviously be included methods of payment and the settlement of piecework prices, proposals to introduce machinery and to sub-divide work differently, suggestions for workshop reorganization, the appointment of foremen and overseers, and the dismissal of workers. The employer or manager would be required to state his case and to produce evidence in favour of it. The workers would not be restricted to the execution of orders coming from above, but would have a voice in the organization and policy both of the workshop and of the industry as a whole.

To those accustomed to think of the present industrial order as the only natural or conceivable system, such a suggestion will seem a preposterous interference with the liberty of the employer. A more important criticism is that this tentative constitutionalism is a tacit admission of the need of more fundamental changes, which, nevertheless, it will do little to promote. It is to be welcomed as a recognition of the necessity of not merely improving the material conditions of the worker, but of altering the whole scheme of relationships upon which industry is based. But it is, at best, a transitional arrangement. The workshop committee, it may be suggested, will have too much power to be welcome to the employer, and too little to satisfy the workers. The employer, if he accepts it, will endeavour to circumscribe its sphere of operations for precisely the same reasons as have caused him to refuse to admit that questions of management are to be settled by collective bargaining with trade unionism. The workers will either find that the workshop committee is the mere illusory concession of a paper constitution, or they will renew the struggle for a larger share in the control of industry from the vantage-ground which such an organization offers. It is, therefore, an illusion to suppose that the scheme which has been indicated offers any promise of diminished industrial friction. Like government which is representative without being responsible, it will strengthen the power of the workers for negative, without substantially increasing it for positive, purposes.

A negative voice in matters of workshop management is better than no voice at all. But there is no finality in the mere systematization of the right of criticism, and its value consists in the opportunity which it offers for a more radical transformation of industrial relationships. That transformation must be found in substituting a relationship of co-ordinate service to the community, for the present subordination of the hired wage-earner to a master who employs him for purposes of profit. The work of the community must be done, and it ought to be done with the aid of the ever-changing improvements made possible by science and invention. If, therefore, the workers are to be able to veto the solution of industrial problems propounded by the employer, their status in industry must be such that they can offer an alternative solution themselves. If they are to resist effectively the types of organization which menace them, they must not merely resist; they must take their part in discovering equally effective types of organization which do not. If they are to exercise corporate freedom, they must be ready to undertake corporate responsibility. The truth is, that both the industrial tyranny denounced by the workers, and the industrial friction and inefficiency deplored by the public, are inseparable from the system under which the employer, instead of being with the workers a fellow-servant of the community, has a direct interest in extracting the maximum of profit from the latter and the maximum of work from the former.

There is no alchemy by which mankind can extract from industry, any more than from the society of nations, a harmony which does not exist within it. Men may be willing to subordinate their interests to a cause or to the community, but they will not surrender those to each other; or, if they yield to *force majeure*, they will be continually in the temper for a *revanche*. While the profiteer and his workers live in a hell of embittered suspicion and call it peace, soldiers are able to face hunger and thirst, cold and heat and intolerable fatigue, because the loss of one is not the gain of another, and because the soul of an army, in spite of all the evils of military life, is comradeship in service. The service is exact because the leadership is disinterested. But if privates were employed for profit by officers, not a man would go over the top. As long as the organization of industry is such that employers can snatch immediate advantages by squeezing the workers and the public, and that workmen see that the immediate advantages of industrial progress pass to their employers, so long will the latter be tyrannical and the former recalcitrant, and so long will the community suffer, and deserve to suffer, from the faults of both, which are also the faults of its own soul.

From that conclusion there is no escape. As are the qualities which men covet, so are the defects which they must endure, for the defects are part of the qualities. If men are fascinated, as they well may be, by the brilliant prizes of plutocracy, they must bear the burden of its limitations. Poverty, economic oppression, and industrial strife are not superficial and transitory incidents of the present industrial order. They are an expression of its essential nature as fundamental as its mechanical perfection and imposing material prizes. Policies, like most modern 'reforms', which accept the permanence of the relationship between hired wage-earner and capitalist employer, and seek merely to modify its effects, may disturb everything, but they will settle nothing. The practical course is not to attempt, by reshuffling the counters, to combine incompatibles; it is to transform the system.

The details of the transformation may be complex, but the principle is simple. It is that, instead of the workers being used by the owners of capital with the object of producing profits for its owners, capital should be used by the workers with the object of producing services for the community. At present, the power of directing industry rests with the owners of capital and their agents. The measure of their success is personal gain; the method by which they attain it is the organization of power, power which is mechanical and power which is human. Reformist movements, whether on the part of the workers or of the State, have acquiesced in that situation and conformed to the strategy which it imposes. Accepting as unalterable the mastery of Capital and the subordination of Labour, they have aimed at limiting the former, or at making the latter less intolerable, by fixing a minimum of wages, sanitation, and education, and a maximum of hours, beyond which the workers should not be driven.

Such a policy is sound in what it attacks and mischievous in what it accepts. For it assumes the relationship between capitalist employer and hired wage-worker, and that relationship itself is a vicious one. It is vicious, because it classifies human beings as a part, and a subordinate part, of the mechanism of production, instead of treating that mechanism merely as an auxiliary to the labour of human beings. As long as that postulate is maintained, it serves as a permanent force to override and pervert all individual reforms which, while leaving it undisturbed on its throne, seek merely to curb its excesses by incidental and external intervention.

What is required is not simply to limit the power of Capital to impose terms upon Labour, but to make the workers, not the capitalist, the centre of industrial authority, subject to such limitations upon their sovereignty as may be imposed in the interests of the community as a whole. It is to employ things in the service of persons, instead of employing persons in the service of things and of the owners of things. The character of modern reformist legislation is, indeed, an indication of the perversion of the relationships to which it is applied. If the human element occupied in industry the position of supremacy and direction which should belong to it, it might be necessary to fix a minimum wage for Capital. It would certainly not be necessary to fix a minimum wage for Labour. For Labour, in conjunction with the community, would determine what part of the product of industry it was worth while to pay in order that sufficient capital might be hired.

Such a reorganization of industry would obviously involve fundamental changes in the relation of employer to worker, and of both to the owner of capital. The employer would cease to be a capitalist or 'master', and would become an organizer, who, as organizer, would take his proper place as one worker among others, and would be, with them, a fellow-servant of the community. The workman would cease to be a 'hand', and would become a citizen of industry, who, like the organizer, had his own special work, and, like the organizer, had a voice in industrial policy and administration. The workers in each industry, including craftsmen, organizers, officials, and scientists, would be responsible to the community, through their representatives, for the service which the whole industry supplied.

The conditions of such a change are, on the one hand, a far higher degree of organization than exists in most industries at the present day, and, on the other hand, the separation of management from ownership. The first can be developed only by the workers within each industry, and though the State can retard, it can do little to hasten, it. The second involves a change in administration which the State, if it pleases, can take the initiative in promoting. But it need not in itself involve a greater revolution, with regard to the legal ownership of land and capital, than occurred when the administration of the railways was three years ago placed in the hands of a council of railway managers acting under the direction of the Government.

Administration would be vested in a joint board composed of representatives of the community, and of all grades of workers in the industry, acting through similarly constituted boards in the different districts into which the industry might naturally be divided. Private 'ownership' would remain, as private ownership remains today in the case of the railways, as long as the public chose to tolerate it. But the ownership of capital is no more inseparable from its administration than the military and judicial functions of a mediaeval feudatory were inseparable from his financial claim to the rents of his peasants; and, if administration were shared between the public and the workers in each industry, the shareholders' interest would be attentuated to a mortgage on the product of the industry. The subordination of workman to master would disappear in their common membership in an association which stood in a direct relation to the community as its organ of industrial administration. If disputes occurred they would be the disagreements of equals, not the bitter warfare of profiteer and proletariat.

Any reorganization of industry must not merely satisfy the demand for industrial freedom; it must also supply the machinery through which the public may secure efficient service. Industry, after all, is a social function, and its reform must not merely promise a higher status to privileged groups, but must carry with it an assurance of the subordination of individual and corporate interests to those of the community. However the principle that industry is a form of public service may be interpreted, there are, at any rate, three implications which are involved in it. The first is, that the community should be offered the best service technically possible at the lowest price compatible with adequate payment to those who provide it. The second is, that when all charges necessary to the supply of a service have been met, any surplus which exists should pass to the community. The third is, that no class should receive an income for which no service is rendered. Vulgar inequality, *privata opulentia et publica egestas*, is the visible evidence of the diversion of industry from the performance of public service to the pursuit of private gain. Instead of the individual being esteemed for his office, the office is esteemed according as it contributes to the riches or advancement of the individual: and this corruption of the purpose of industry results in privilege, as the debasement of the organization of industry involves oppression.

Now, in a healthy society, the right authority to hold industry to its proper character of a social function are the persons engaged in it. It is sometimes suggested that if its policy were controlled by those who make things, and not by those who judge it by figures in a balance-sheet and quotations on a market, its quality of a public service would tend to be maintained by the dislike of commercial chicanery, which is natural to most men who make a living by working, and not by buying and selling the work of other people. Whether this is so or not, it is clear that industry ought to be professionalized, in the sense of being governed by standards other than the immediate advantage of the particular individuals or companies who compose it. In matters of price and quality, the public has a right to be protected against the unfair practices of the craft, and the members of the craft have a right to be protected against the unfair practices of one another.

Nor is there anything impracticable in such an ideal, however remote it may appear to be from the tendencies of the modern commercial world. It need not be pretended that corporate selfishness can be exorcised by professional rules. What can be created is a corporate conscience, which may be sensitive or indifferent, but to which an appeal on public and moral grounds is possible. There have been ages in which the professions both of medicine and of teaching were rather a mean speculation upon public credulity. And if, while the former has got rid of the quack, and the latter of Squeers, the manufacturer still denies the possibility of applying ethical standards to his own calling, and placates his conscience with the maxim that 'Business is business', the reason is certainly not that there is anything more sordid in the occupations which are called trades than there is in the occupations which are called professions. Compared with that of a barrister, the work of building a house, or extracting coal, or manufacturing cotton piece-goods, is a school of morals. It is certainly no meaner in itself than is that of attending the sick or instructing the ignorant. It is as necessary, and therefore it is as honourable. Given an organization of production in which the direction of it was shared between the workers and the community, it would be as possible to work out a code of public honour and recognized obligations in industries as it has been in the professions.

If the conception of industry as a social function is to be effective, it must, then, be a spirit working within it not merely a body of rules imposed by an external authority. But, in the revolution needed to make the development of that spirit a possibility, the State can, if it pleases, play a considerable part. In the first place, it can insist that industry shall be conducted upon a basis of complete publicity, except in so far as paramount national interests make publicity undesirable in exceptional cases. If industry is carried on to serve the public, not merely for the personal profit of those who supply the capital for it, the community has the right to satisfy itself that the service is faithfully discharged. Unless there is complete publicity with regard to profits and costs, it is impossible to form any judgment either of the reasonableness of the prices which are charged or of the claims to remuneration of the different parties engaged in production. In the present ignorance of these crucial elements in the economic situation, most industrial disputes are battles in the dark, where 'ignorant armies clash by night'.

On more than one occasion even during the war, when honourable men might reasonably be reluctant to take advantage of public necessities, both the Government and the private consumer have been charged prices which bore no relation to the cost of production. It is notorious, indeed, that the somewhat tardy adoption of the practice of requiring contractors to submit costings to justify their quotations, has saved large sums to the public purse. There is no reason why those sums should not continue to be saved in time of peace. There is no reason why an Industrial Department should not audit the accounts of all companies, and issue regular reports on the cost of production in different industries, which would enable the public to check the prices quoted. It is a commonplace of democracy that publicity is the best guarantee against political abuses. It should be used as a safeguard against economic abuses. It should be the duty of a government department concerned with industry to publish full reports showing the amount and distribution of the profits made by different trades, and by the individual firms composing them. If it is the case, as is often alleged, that the profits in most industries are inconsiderable, they ought to be known in the interests both of the shareholders and of industrial peace. If they are excessive, they should be known in the interests of the workers and of the public.

But publicity, after all, is no more than an antiseptic. If industry is to be conducted as the honourable social function which it should be, it must not merely escape from its rather humiliating tradition of secrecy. Its subordination to the public service must be so direct as to be unmistakable; and the first condition of such subordination is that it should cease to be burdened with payments which are disproportionate to the service rendered, or which are made for no service at all. It must be delivered from the domination of the *rentier*. For charges which are in the nature of economic rent, or monopoly profits, or which are made merely because one party in industry is in a strong position to corner the market or to drive a bargain, there is no more moral or economic justification than there was for the *lods et ventes*, or *banalités*, or *vingtaines* of the old *régime*.

They lower the economic vitality of society by a double process of exhaustion. On the one hand, they are a mere tax on the community, a tax which is paid to private persons instead of to the State. On the other hand, they enable their recipients to exercise a demand which diverts to the supply of luxuries productive power which would otherwise be directed to the multiplication of the necessaries of common humanity, so that the classes thus endowed wear several men's clothes, eat several men's dinners, occupy several men's homes, and live several men's lives. The business men and politicians who regard the problem of reconstruction as concerned primarily with intensifying the productivity of industry, may be invited to consider the energy which would be set free for the production of things indispensable, if there were no demand to divert capital and labour into the manufacture of private motor-cars, private yachts, rich men's houses and expensive hotels.

The economic waste of functionless incomes is considerable, and in a world that will be obliged, like a platoon of soldiers, to sweat for its daily rations, that waste will be felt more severely than in the age of easy-going affluence which ended in 1914. But, compared with their effect on the *morale* of the community, the mere economic burden of the pensioners of industry is almost trivial. There is much talk at present of the necessity of increasing productive energy. But one condition of more strenuous production is an alteration in distribution. No man will work harder to make necessaries, if he sees that another obtains comforts without working at all. As long as any considerable part of the actual output of wealth goes to classes who, however individually meritorious, have not laboured to produce it, so long will that fact serve as a perpetual discouragement to effort on the part of those who have. The surest way to encourage production is to make it clear that those who do not produce will not consume.

The right principle for the community to follow is simple, though its application may be complex. Though industrial reform cannot be imposed by the State, the State can, at least, emphasize the principle that industry and trade are a form of public service, and that the man who in time of peace plays on public necessities to amass a fortune—the monopolist, or the speculator who corners the market, or the urban landlord who grows rich by other men's industry—is morally on a par with the merchant or manufacturer who holds his countrymen to ransom in time of war. It should, therefore, encourage those types of economic organization which are likely, by their constitution, to put efficient service before considerations of profit. It should discourage those which are not. And it should regard incomes to which no function is annexed, or which exceed any reasonable interpretation of the necessities of healthy existence, as the proper object of special taxation.

Economy and efficiency are not the last words in industry. It is more important that its organization should be such as to offer the worker what has been called above, the conditions of corporate freedom, than that it should function with a mechanical efficiency, if efficiency can be purchased only by an inhuman rigidity of discipline. But, on their own plane, economy and efficiency are important; and, happily, the choice between these qualities and the control by the workers of all grades over the day-to-day administration of the industry is not one which need be made. Indeed, what impedes such a reorganization of the greater industries on the basis of corporate self-government is precisely the industrial autocracy which, there is reason to believe, also prejudices the services which they offer to the public. To that extent freedom and function go together, and every measure which makes the coal mines or the railways the property of the community would, at least, facilitate, though by itself it would not ensure, wider opportunities of industrial self-government to miners and railwaymen.

In maintaining and extending its control over industry, the community could, therefore, meet the demands both of the worker and of the consumer. It need not choose between subjecting the former to a new clerkocracy and leaving the latter at the mercy of competition qualified by more or less monopolistic combinations. What it can do, is to maintain the interest of the general public in sound and efficient service, while leaving the maximum liberty to those in the industry to determine how exactly the service shall be organized. If it adopts this standpoint, it will naturally not abandon the claim to a kind of eminent domain over industry which has been established during the war, but which had, in fact, been in gradual preparation long before the war began. It will continue, by organizing the supply of raw materials, to secure for industry, the advantages of large scale purchases, and incidentally, by eliminating speculation, to confine the employer to his proper function of a specialist in industrial administration. And it will continue to treat the railways and mines as public services. But it will devolve as large a share of administration as possible upon those actually engaged in the industries.

Such reforms imply a change in the public attitude, not only towards labour, but towards property. And, in the England which existed before the war, to touch property was to sport with lions. Mankind is moving in uncharted waters, and is as likely to exaggerate, as to underestimate, the change in its psychology induced by the voyage. It is possible that the pathetic instinct to demand payment for privilege, as though it were a kind of service, will re-emerge jaunty and unrepentant out of the sea of blood and tears in which it has been temporarily submerged, and that in a world where not a few have given all, there may still be classes and individuals whose ideal is not to give but to take. Such claims, if they are made, may be regarded with pity, but without apprehension. Men who have endured the rigours of war in order to make the world safe for democracy, will find ways of overcoming the social forces and institutions which threaten that cause in time of peace.

9

THE NATIONALIZATION OF THE COAL
INDUSTRY[1]

I. INTRODUCTORY

Up to 1919 it might fairly be said that the nationalization of
foundation industries was an aspiration rather than a policy.
The principle of public ownership had long been accepted by
the Labour Movement, and had been broadened in recent
years by the declaration that the workers' organizations must
share with the State the control of industry. But it was still an
article of faith rather than a programme worked out, as a
programme must be, with the elaboration of detail needed to
make it an immediate practical issue. It was attacked or
defended in general terms. The majority of its supporters were
more conversant with its social advantages than with the
technical problems which, whatever its social advantages, it
would have to meet and solve. To the common sense of ordinary
citizens who were not fired with any conception of a new social
order, it appeared hardly more significant than the proposal
to establish a channel tunnel or to build a new dam on the
Nile. They read that the Trades Union Congress had passed a
resolution in favour of nationalization with the same uninterested equanimity as they read that an astronomer had
discovered canals on Mars, and regarded the former as hardly
more relevant to their own concerns than the latter.

The Government and the propertied interests took full
advantage of that indifference. Once political democracy has
been established, privileged classes retain their position, not
by a frontal resistance on burning social issues, but by preventing social issues from ever becoming a burning question. A
century of experience has made the English plutocracy a past

[1] From a Labour Party pamphlet, 1919.

118

master of the strategy which consists in 'refusing the centre'. Down to 1919, it had contrived, with almost unbroken success, to keep the question of public ownership and democratic control out of the region in which it would necessitate a declaration of policy, determine the alignment of parties, and influence a general election.

The events of the last year in the Mining Industry[1] have brought that social strategy to an end. Henceforward no government and no party will be able to pretend that nationalization is one of the questions with regard to which politicians can keep what they are fond of describing as an 'open mind'. It will be impossible to assert in the future that it is a wanton disturbance of a smoothly running industrial system, or that it is a 'mere theory' with no solid body of economic and technical argument behind it. The action of the miners, endorsed by organized Labour through the Trades Union Congress, in making it part of their immediate industrial programme has destroyed the first position; the evidence before the Commission has destroyed the second. Both together have brought the question out of the region of generalities into one where immediate decisions are inevitable.

For the first time, the evidence for and against capitalism in one great industry has been marshalled and presented to the public, not by private individuals, but by a public body appointed by Act of Parliament. For the first time, its economic wastefulness has been remorselessly laid bare, not by reformers, but by technical experts, administrators, men of science and officials, including two blameless baronets whom the mine-owners found it hardest to forgive. For the first time, *all* the business men on a Commission, not directly concerned in the industry under investigation, have affirmed that 'the present system of ownership and working . . . stands condemned, and some other system must be substituted for it'. For the first time, the case for transferring to public ownership property worth not less than £135,000,000, and the methods by which, when transferred, it is to be administered, have been worked

[1] The Miners' Federation accepted nationalization of the mines as their policy and a distinguished Government Commission under Mr Justice Sankey (including R. H. Tawney among its members) also proposed that the mining industry should be transferred to public ownership. It took all but thirty years and a powerful Labour Government to put these proposals into effect.—Ed.

out in detail not by socialists, but by that most venerable of British institutions, a judge of the High Court. Nor, when capitalism is dead, will bureaucracy be its heir. As far as the coal industry is concerned, that spectre, which the Government and the interests behind it have dressed up again to terrify the innocent public into continuing the system which fleeces it, has been laid for ever. The proposals, both of Mr Justice Sankey and the Miners' Federation, will have the effect of setting up a decentralized system under which the management of the industry in each coal-field will rest in the hands of practical men with local knowledge and experience, and on which both consumer and worker will have representation.

The result upon public opinion has been revolutionary. It has shown that directly even men biased by tradition in favour of private enterprise are brought into close contact with the detailed conditions of one great industry, they find capitalism, on public grounds, intolerable. It has made impossible for ever a repetition of the dramatic gesture with which the capitalist used to pose as the guardian and agent of the interests of the community—'strike me, but spare the public'. It has confirmed the arguments of the workers, and has brought public owner-ship and democratic control into the field, not as remote possibilities, but as the only way of extricating the nation from an intolerable *impasse*. No one hereafter can say that, even if capitalism in the coal industry is tyrannical and inhuman, at least it is efficient, or that private enterprise must be main-tained in the interests of the consumer, or that free competition (when it existed) cut down to the bare minimum the profits of producing and distributing coal, or that nationalization necessarily involves 'bureaucracy' and 'over-centralization', or that public ownership and democratic management are impracticable.

One by one, the defences of the present system were reconnoitred and overthrown, not by the miners or their colleagues, but by witnesses whose independence was above suspicion. One by one, the arguments for public ownership were examined, criticized, and found unanswerable. The consequence is that the policy of nationalization occupies today a position of vantage which it has never held in the past. The burden of proof no longer rests upon its supporters, but upon its opponents. The case for it has been made out. What is needed now is that the general public should master it, and should end a situation which is as objectionable from the standpoint of the consumer of coal as it is from that of the mine-workers.[1]

II. THE ADVANTAGES OF PUBLIC OWNERSHIP

'Nationalization' has more than one meaning, and is compatible with several different types of organization. The principles which should determine the administration of the coal industry are discussed below. Provided, however, that the obvious pitfalls of bureaucracy and over-centralization, which are as familiar to the advocates of nationalization as to its critics, are avoided, the advantages of public ownership are immense. It will benefit the consumer by making possible the elimination of the various sources of waste, the cost of which is at present reflected in the price of coal. It will benefit the mine-worker by removing the downward pressure of capitalism on his standard of life, by making room for considerations of social well-being which are at present subordinated to the pursuit of dividends, and by securing him an effective voice in the policy and organization of the industry. Nor is the least of its advantages that by making the most fundamental of all industries a public service carried on in partnership between the State and the workers, it will call into operation motives of public spirit and professional zeal which are at present stifled by the subordination of the industry to the pursuit of private gain, and which will raise the whole tone and quality of our industrial civilization.

How costly to the consumer, and how tyrannical to the mine-worker the conduct of the coal industry has been in the past, has been shown in the short analysis of it given in the preceding pages.[2] As far as the consumer is concerned, the most

---

[1] Tawney then analysed in detail the pre-1914 organization of the coal industry, the 'control' of the industry by the Government during the 1914–18 war, and the shortcomings of this policy, the wretched wages and conditions of the miners, the exploitation of the consumers, and the anarchy in coal distribution. He then discusses, only to dismiss, alternatives to public ownership which were then receiving attention. These sections have no contemporary relevance, and are omitted.

[2] The omitted sections.

obvious advantages of public ownership, accompanied by a democratic system of administration, are summarized below. It should be observed that they do not repose upon the assumption that any preternatural degree of intelligence will be displayed by the personnel of a nationalized system—an assumption which, since such a system will naturally employ many, if not most, of the existing officials, would clearly be illegitimate. They are of a kind which a public and representative body, of its very nature, possesses, and which private ownership (whatever its other merits) cannot pretend to cultivate. Such a body can handle the problem of organizing production and distribution as a whole, instead of piecemeal. It can wait, and need not snatch at immediate profit at the cost of prejudicing the future of the industry. It can enlist on its side motives to which the private profit-maker (if he is aware of their existence) cannot appeal. It can put the welfare of human beings, worker and consumer, first.

Thus:

(a) Owing to the differences in the character and accessibility of the coal worked by different collieries, a 'price that is a fortune for one colliery is bankruptcy for another'.[1] The financial unification of the industry in public hands will secure that the surplus gains of the more favourably situated mines accrue, not to functionless shareholders, but to the community.

(b) As long as the mines are worked with a single eye to private profit, the mineral resources of the nation tend to be exploited recklessly, through the 'creaming' of pits, and the failure to work the less profitable seams. Under public ownership, mines will be worked with a due regard to the conversation of what is the most important source of mineral wealth. 'Under a system of collective production artificial factors which impede mining would be removed. Owing to the extinction of the competition prevalent in normal times between rival owners, coal, good and inferior, could be worked together, instead of bringing up only that which is necessary to allow of one owner competing with another.'

(c) At present, much coal is lost in barriers between different properties, and, because of the failure of owners to co-operate in drainage schemes, valuable tracts of coal are liable to be

---

[1] All the quotations are from the Report of the Coal Industry Commission, 1919.

drowned out. Public ownership will save part (though not all) of the barriers now necessary, and will make possible the establishment of central pumping stations 'at the most advantageous points, with considerable resultant saving in cost'.

(*d*) Once the different mines in a district form part of a single system, they will reap the economies arising from common buying of materials and common selling of the product. 'The material annually consumed by the collieries of the United Kingdom is enormous. It must be apparent that some 1,500 concerns purchasing materials independently cannot do so as effectively or cheaply as if they were one concern.'

(*e*) Administration and managerial expenses will be diminished, as they are normally diminished when businesses combine which formerly competed, and the larger unit will make possible the more economical use of technical knowledge and ability. 'Economy of administration in this respect is obvious. The number of directors would be greatly reduced, as also the number of managing directors, consulting engineers, and general managers. The middleman would largely disappear.'

(*f*) Knowledge will be pooled, and an improvement introduced into one mine will be available for the service as a whole. 'Assuming that each station on a railway system was left free to evolve its own destiny, without control from a central authority or headquarters, we should get something akin to the system of separate units which obtains in coal-mining.'

(*g*) Instead of the financial position of each colliery being concealed as far as possible from its competitors and from the mine-workers, there will be complete publicity with regard to the cost both of getting coal in each pit and in each district, and of distributing it to the consumer. Hence the public for the first time will know exactly what items enter into the price charged it for coal, and will be able to judge whether that price is reasonable or not. In the words of Mr Justice Sankey, 'The other industries and the consumers generally will have a voice in deciding the amount of coal to be produced and the price at which it is sold, *which they have not had in the past*'. The mine-workers will know exactly what profits are being made, and the suspicions inseparable from secrecy will thus be removed. The bodies administering the industry will be able to compare the costs of getting and distributing coal in different pits and districts, and will thus be in a position to insist on the abolition of uneconomical methods and on the levelling up of the system of production and distribution throughout the industry.

(*h*) The equipment of the more backward mines, which at present, standing by themselves, find it difficult to raise the capital needed for the introduction of improvements, will be brought to the level of the rest. 'The present system of numerous separate ownerships militates against it (i.e. improvement). Under a system of collective production . . . capital would be available to allow of the smaller concerns adopting labour-saving appliances to a greater extent than at present. This is one of the directions in which the present system of numerous small entities (as against a combination of interests) is wasteful and extravagant.'

(*i*) The waste arising from the separate ownership of trucks would come to an end. 'The present system of private ownership of wagons is obviously wasteful. There are some 700,000 privately-owned railway wagons hampering the railway companies by reason of special shunting and marshalling of the railway stock. The system also has the effect of increasing colliery costs owing to the amount of shunting they have to do.'

(*j*) The super-power stations which are to be erected, and the public railway service, which, it is to be presumed, will be established shortly, will necessarily purchase immense quantities of coal. The public ownership of coal mines is the only certain way of protecting these services, and through them the consumer, against exploitation by 'rings' of coal producers.

(*k*) The middlemen who at present intervene between the producer of coal and the consumer, to the number of three or even of four, will be replaced by a system under which coal for household purposes will be distributed in each area by the Local Authorities. Its price will be fixed at a level sufficient to cover costs, and will not be raised, as now, whenever a 'cold snap' make it possible to squeeze the market. The saving to the consumer of coal which such an organization would make possible has been already established by the experience of Co-operative Societies.

(*l*) If the principles suggested below are observed, it is reasonable to hope that the coal supply of the country will not be interrupted by the friction between workers and employers which, whether it flares up into formal disputes or not, is at all times a grave economic loss, and that the community as a whole will gain in so far as the change in the status of the mine-worker causes their experience and professional pride to be enlisted in the improvement of the industry.

These are all advantages which will accrue, in the first instance, to the consumer. It is evident, indeed, that in so far as the more efficient and economical conduct of the industry enables the cost of supplying coal to be reduced, a fund is created in which the mine-worker may be expected to share. It is not, however, so much in the direct additions which it would make to his income, as in the cessation of petty tyrannies, the increase in the provision for health and safety, and in the greater freedom and security offered by his new status as a partner with the State in the conduct of the industry, that the benefits of nationalization to the mine-worker are to be found.

Thus:

(*a*) Given public ownership and the system of administration which is outlined below, the worker will be protected against the various devices by which a sharp or unscrupulous management endeavours to cut down his earnings. Attention will be concentrated on reducing the real cost of production by improvements in organization, and by the elimination of waste, not, as often now, on reducing prices for cutting coal to a point at which only the strongest worker, by almost inhuman toil, can keep off the minimum, and on increasing profits at the expense of wages, while leaving the cost of production unaltered.

(*b*) Provisions for health and safety will no longer be enforced from outside upon managers whose primary concern, however personally humane and careful they may desire to be, is necessarily to make the business as profitable as possible from the point of view of the shareholders. The diminution of the dangers incidental to mining will be a primary duty of the authorities responsible for administering a national system. Given continuous concentration on that problem, without the conflict of interests which the pursuit of profit inevitably involves, it is reasonable to expect that the nation will obtain its coal without killing between three and four miners every day, or injuring 160,000 every year.

(c) The arduousness of the mine-workers' toil can be considerably reduced by the introduction, wherever possible, of the latest machinery and equipment, such as already exists in the most up-to-date mines, but which, according to the evidence laid before the Commission, is woefully lacking in the remainder. Every practical man knows that the strain of the miner's work can be enormously diminished, provided that a serious effort is made with that object. Men could be conveyed near to their working places, for example, far more generally than is the case at present. It is a common saying that the fatigue of walking to and from the working place, often for two miles or more and up and down steep inclines, is more exhausting than work at the face itself. In some districts it is paid for; in others, not. And, of course, the working time lost means a lower output of coal. Intelligent management would face the immediate cost of providing means of conveyance, wherever practicable. Again, the general introduction of hand electric lamps (in addition, of course, to the ordinary safety lamp) would relieve the strain on the eyes, which is one cause of nystagmus, and would also increase safety by facilitating a more thorough examination of the roof than is often possible at present.

(d) The irregularity of employment, which at present results in the average working year of miners being less than 280 days, may be expected to be replaced by almost complete continuity, when the mines, instead of competing with each other for orders, are operated as units in a single system.

(e) The social conditions of the mining industry, in particular the appalling scandal of miners' houses, the failure to provide pithead baths, the absence of any system of holidays on full wages or of pensions, are not likely to be tolerated when the mines have passed into public ownership.

(f) Most important of all, the mine-workers themselves will be in a position of responsibility and power which will secure, not only that their practical experience is placed at the service of the community, but that the industry shall be conducted with full consideration for the human interests of all concerned in it. Through the machinery of pit committees, district councils, and national mining council, they will be able to suggest measures for improving both the quality of the service and the conditions under which the mining population works and lives. They will no longer be 'hands', employed for the advantage of a profit-making company, but partners in a communal enterprise. It is impossible to exaggerate the significance of that change of status. It is the difference between freedom and something like serfdom.

III. THE ORGANIZATION OF THE SERVICE

The efficiency of the public mining service will depend, once national ownership is established, upon the character of the administrative machinery established for the conduct of the industry. Public ownership, indeed, however administered, can hardly fail to eliminate some of the graver abuses which are inseparable from the present system of leaving the production of coal to be carried on for the profit of shareholders in some 1,500 separate companies, and its distribution to the self-interest of successive tiers of middlemen. Mere unification will inevitably reduce the wastes involved in the separate ownership and administration of mines, and will secure the surplus reaped by the more productive or better-situated collieries for the advantage of the community. Nor is it credible that, once the community has a direct responsibility for the welfare of the mining population, it will tolerate the continuance of the grave scandals of accidents, housing, and bad social conditions, which shocked the public conscience when they were revealed by the Coal Industry Commission.

But considerable as are the benefits to be anticipated from the mere transference of the industry to public ownership, they are not by themselves the most that the nation has a right to expect. It ought not to be satisfied merely with establishing an organization which is preferable to the present system—a task, in view of the *débâcle* of capitalism in the coal industry, not difficult of achievement. It must aim not only at eliminating the gross and obvious defects of private ownership, but at avoiding the mistakes which have prejudiced public ownership itself in the past, and of combining in the new organization which it establishes all the safeguards of efficiency and humanity which experience and forethought can suggest. It is not enough, in short, merely to insist upon public ownership, however true it may be that public ownership is the one policy which opens a road through the present *impasse*. Public ownership is compatible with several different methods of administration. What is necessary now is to secure that a fair chance is given it by insisting that the system of administration adopted shall be the best.

The objections which the 'plain man' entertains to nationalization may be expressed in half a dozen words. They are official inertia, red tape, over-centralization, the 'Civil Service tradition'. Now these objections are often justified. But what the plain man ought to realize is, that they are the very alphabet of the subject, that the qualities for which those words stand are disliked at least as much by the miners as they are by him, that the necessity of preventing their dominance in a nationalized coal industry is almost the first thought which occurs to any advocate of nationalization, and that the proposals both of the Miners' Federation and of Mr Justice Sankey are carefully designed to avert the dangers associated in the past with bureaucratic administration. It may be argued, of course, that they have failed to do so, just as those who at present administer the industry have failed conspicuously to safeguard it from the even more serious defects incidental to the private control of a great foundation service. But if they have failed, it is not through inability or unwillingness to appreciate the points which require special attention. Before, therefore, the critic allows the word 'nationalization' to throw him into an apoplexy, he will be well advised to consider what exactly 'nationalization', as interpreted by the Miners' Federation and by Mr Justice Sankey, means.

There are certain differences between the original programme of the Federation and that contained in the report of the Chairman of the Coal Industry Commission. But it will be seen that, once public ownership is established, both of them rest, broadly speaking, on two main principles. The first is decentralized administration within the framework of a national system. There is no question of 'managing the industry from Whitehall'. The characteristics of different coal-fields vary so widely that a manager who is competent in one may be almost helpless in another, until he has learned how to deal with its peculiarities. Local knowledge and experience are, in fact, essential, and it is to local knowledge and experience that both the Miners' Federation and Mr Justice Sankey propose to entrust the administration of the industry.

The constitution which they recommend is—to borrow a term from political science—not 'unitary' but 'federal'. There will be a division of functions and powers between the Central Authority and District Authorities. The former will lay down general rules as to those matters which must necessarily be dealt with on a national basis. The latter will administer the industry within their own Districts, and as long as they comply with those rules, and supply their quota of coal, will possess local autonomy, and will follow the method of working the pits which they think best suited to local conditions. This plan is in accordance with existing mining practice. It corresponds to the organization of the workers, which has the coal-field as its basis and bond of union. It is in line with the spirit and tradition of English Local Government.

The second principle is that the responsibility for the conduct of the industry shall be shared between representatives of the community and representatives of the workers. Under both schemes there would be (a) a Minister of Mines responsible to Parliament, (b) a central Mining Council working in co-operation with him, (c) District Mining Councils controlling production and distribution in the main coal-fields, the number suggested by Mr Justice Sankey being fourteen, (d) Pit Committees, composed of the representatives of the workers at each particular pit. Under both schemes these authorities would be composed in such a way as to be representative of the main interests concerned in the production and distribution of coal, the State, the consumers (industrial and household), scientific and technical experts and the mine-workers.

The precise amount of representation to be accorded to the different interests concerned is obviously a matter of degree: the essential thing is that the authorities responsible for the conduct of the industry should be composed, not of officials, but of men of practical experience, and in such a way as to secure that the views both of producers and of consumers receive attention. Not less important, they would secure also that the industry commanded the best expert and scientific knowledge available. It may be anticipated, for example, that the National Mining Council would include, in addition to representatives of consumers and mineworkers, persons with expert knowledge as to, at any rate (*a*) mining geology and practice; (*b*) finance; (*c*) health and safety; (*d*) housing; (*e*) the commercial side of the business and the distribution of coal. Under such an authority, it would hardly continue to be—as it now is—the case, that no complete or accurate record was kept of trial sinkings, or that preventible dangers were not removed, or that the housing conditions of colliery districts remained what in certain parts of Great Britain they were proved before the Commission to be, or that coal passed through the hands of three or four distributors on its way to the household consumer.

IV. HOW PUBLIC OWNERSHIP WOULD WORK

Assuming some such machinery to be established, how would it work? The function of the National Mining Council would be to deal with the large questions of policy affecting the industry as a whole, for example finance, the surveying of the coal-fields and boring for coal, the opening of new mines, the determination of the total amount of coal to be produced, the organization of an economical and efficient system of distribution, prices and national wages question, general regulations with regard to health and safety, and the allocation of a fund for housing in mining districts. The District Mining Councils would be responsible for meeting, in accordance with the special conditions of their respective districts, the demands made upon them by the National Mining Council, and for carrying out its general policy. They would carry on the routine administration of their own coal-fields, would settle the most efficient way of getting coal in the special circumstances of their various localities, would be responsible for the equipment and output of mines in their areas, would determine where pumping or generating stations should be erected, would appoint managers, would see that each pit supplied the quota that could reasonably be demanded from it, would secure regularity of production, and would be a court of appeal to which questions from individual pits could be referred. The Pit Committees would not relieve the manager of his legal responsibility, which must remain as it is at present. But they would assist him in dealing with questions of discipline, of health and safety, and of output. They would suggest improvements in methods of working and would point to sources of waste which could be removed. They would, in short, be the organ through which the views of the men in each particular mine found expression, and through which the workers took their share both in the effective discharge of their obligations to the community and in the control of the conditions upon which their own well-being depends.

The distributive side of the industry, which is at present in anarchy, would undergo a corresponding reorganization. The 600,000 or 700,000 privately owned trucks, belonging to some thousand separate collieries and merchants, which are empty for half their lives and hamper the railways with needless shunting, would be pooled in the hands of a public service, and would, of course, be used indifferently for all collieries. Instead of household coal passing through the hands of three or more distributors before it reaches the consumer, the District Mining Councils would arrange to supply the Local Authorities in the area allotted them with their quota of coal, and the Local Authorities would distribute it direct to the household consumer. In the event of the users of coal, whether industrial or household, having any complaint to make as to the quantity or quality supplied to them, or the price charged, they would be free to address their complaints to the District Mining Council (on which they would be represented), and, failing redress there, to the National Mining Council (on which they would also be represented). They could raise the question further on the Fuel Consumers' Council, which it is proposed under the Federation's Bill to establish, and the Council could in turn approach the Minister of Mines. In view of the complete helplessness of the ordinary household consumer when confronted with a rise of price hitherto, and of the well-known fact that collieries and distributors took advantage of every threatened dispute or cold snap to raise prices against him, there is something cynically comic in the suggestion that he has anything but an immense increase in influence and in power of self-protection to gain from public ownership, accompanied by a scheme of administration such as is suggested above. How the coal-owners, who are now posing as Protectors of the Poor, regard the consumer can be illustrated shortly from the following dialogue, which took place between Lord Gainford, the principal witness on behalf of the Mining Association, and a member of the Commission:

'Has it not occurred to you that if you make the workmen anxious to increase the profits and to share the profits with the owners, the workmen may combine with the owners to exploit the general public?'

'I think the general public who consume the coal will take very good care that they do not pay more for the coal than the industry in which they are engaged can afford to pay.'

'How do you suggest to secure that? You have suggested no protection whatever.'

'Because the consumer, as soon as you raise the price against him, declines to become a purchaser.'

'The ordinary household may go without a fire in winter, but is that a very satisfactory way of bringing the men and the coal-owners to a sense of their duty?'

'It brings them very much up against the proposition that the whole of their livelihood depends upon the output of coal, and they will have to supply it at a price which the consumer is ready to pay.'

'Then the only remedy you propose is that there should be a consumers' strike?'

'That is it.'

In place of the 'consumers' strike' advocated by Lord Gainford as a remedy for exorbitant prices, the scheme of administration outlined above offers (a) representation to the consumers of coal on the authorities representing the industry; (b) a Consumers' Council; (c) a Minister responsible to Parliament at the head of the whole system. It is not difficult to judge which plan offers consumers the best guarantee that their interests will be considered.

Nor does the other aspect of the problem of distribution, the export of coal, which is sometimes thought to be the crux of nationalization, offer any insoluble problem. If it were the case that the export trade presented difficulties too great to be handled under nationalization, one possible course would be to leave it in private hands. As long as the exporter gets his coal at a price which will enable him to sell it abroad, it does not matter to him whether he buys it from a public colliery or from a private owner. In fact, however, large profits are made on the export of coal, and it would hardly be tolerable that private merchants should buy public coal cheap and sell it abroad at the highest price that it would fetch.

On the whole, therefore, the argument is in favour of nationalizing the export trade. Either the Public Mines Department could itself step into the place of the exporters and export coal in bulk, much as the War Contracts Department during the war imported wool and other commodities in bulk, or it could employ the existing exporting merchants on a commission. The suggestion that, by undertaking the export business, the State would become involved in complications with foreign powers, betrays an amazing *naïveté* as to the present situation. The State is up to the hilt in these complications already, for foreign powers are not so innocent as to suppose that it escapes responsibility merely because the profits from high export prices pass to private traders. If it were thought well that a public department should undertake the export of coal, the only difference would be that the State's responsibility would become obvious and formal, instead of being concealed behind the vested interests of exporters.

It is too much, perhaps, to expect that critics should burn their arsenal of controversial literature. But, in view of the nature of the schemes now put forward, that of Mr Justice Sankey as well as that of the Miners' Federation, the greater part of it is as obsolete as the armaments of the Stone Age. There will be no 'over-centralization', for the keynote of both sets of proposals is decentralization, and an authority composed of men who know the special conditions of each district will be responsible for the conduct of the industry in it, not distant officials in Whitehall. There will be no 'hide-bound bureaucracy', for both expressly provide that the official shall be controlled by men of practical experience. There will be no 'Civil Service incompetence', for they break with the civil service traditions, and Mr Justice Sankey goes so far as to recommend that 'the present civil service system of selection and promotion by length of service, of grades of servants, of minuting opinions and reports from one servant to another, and of salaries and pensions, shall not apply to the servants attached to the Mines Department'. There will be no 'Treasury control', for both schemes provided for the financial independence of the mining industry. There will be no 'exploitation of the public by the producers', for both schemes provide for the responsibility of the service to Parliament, and for the representation of the consumers.

The idea that public ownership *necessarily* involves red tape, centralization, officialdom, is, in fact, an illusion. It *may* suffer from these vices, if it is organized so as to encourage them, just as privately managed industries (for example, the railways) may suffer from them, and from certain others as well. It *need* not do so, if care is taken to avoid them. The evils of bureaucracy have been so frequently emphasized, have been brought home so insistently of recent years, and are so distasteful to the workers themselves, that to take precautions against them is almost the first point which occurs to anyone who is today drafting a scheme of public ownership.

In the proposals both of the miners and of Mr Justice Sankey those dangers are deliberately recognized, and measures are proposed for averting them. A body in each coal-field, not a remote authority in London, will be responsible for getting and distributing coal in its area. The management of the industry will be vested in the hands of practical men, and represent both the producers of coal and its consumers. Indeed, were either of these schemes adopted, it would be in their hands far more completely than it is today, when considerations of productive efficiency are liable to be overridden by the financial interests of owners of minerals and shareholders in mines. The difference between its conduct under public ownership and its conduct today is threefold. In the first place, it would be administered, not in order to pay dividends, but in order to provide an economical service of coal for the public. In the second place, each unit would be part of a team, and would not aim at cutting its neighbour's throat. In the third place, the workers themselves would have a direct responsibility for its efficiency, and sufficient power to make that responsibility a reality.

V. INDUSTRIAL DEMOCRACY

It is impossible to exaggerate the importance of the last condition. No scheme for reorganizing the coal industry can be regarded as even approximately satisfactory which does not offer those engaged in it an effective voice in the control of its policy and administration. The immediate gain to the workers from such a participation in the government of the industry upon which their livelihood depends is obvious and direct. Through Pit Committees, they will deal with questions of discipline, of output, of safety, health and comfort in each individual mine. On the District Council and National Mining Council they will review not only the social policy of the industry, its wages, hours, safety, and conditions in respect of health and housing, but the technical and commercial conditions which govern its development, and will do so, not as mere critics, but as men who can translate their ideals and experience into practice, and who bear the liability for making them a success. The individual workman will know that the authority responsible for administering the industry consists, in part, of men with the same experience as himself, and that he, by his own suggestions and criticisms, can improve the working conditions and efficiency of his own pit. The organization of which he is a member will no longer be concerned solely with resisting reductions or securing advances. It will form part of the government of the industry, and will thus be in a position to assume, as it cannot now, a professional responsibility for the quality of the service.

The advantages of increased safety, leisure, security of employment, health and comfort, are not the only benefits by which such a change in status will be accompanied. The absence of these things from the lives of all but a minority of mankind is a monstrous evil. But it is an evil which is a symptom of a more deeply rooted and inveterate disease, and will disappear only with the removal of the cause which produces it. That cause is the government of industry, which means the government of all who work in it, by the agents of shareholders for the pecuniary gain of shareholders. In a word, it is capitalism. 'Capital', as industry is organized today, hires 'labour'. It rubs its hands if 'labour' is 'cheap' and 'docile'. It cries and cuts itself with knives if 'labour' is 'dear' or 'restive'. It allows the workers as much initiative and responsibility as pit-ponies, and scraps them, with other worn-out tools, when they have served its purpose.

Such an industrial order, and the social system which reposes on it, whatever its economic consequences, is essentially servile. It involves the treatment of human beings as part of the apparatus of production, instead of as the end for which alone it is worth while to carry on production at all. It means that the working lives of whole populations are dependent upon the will of half a dozen directors. It is, in short, the enemy of freedom. It is freedom which the miners, and not only the miners but other bodies of workers, both in Great Britain and in the United States, are now demanding. They claim as a moral right—and many mine-managers, though they dare not say so, agree with them—the power to manage their own working lives, to take part with the community in the government of their own profession, and to serve the great body of their fellow-countrymen, not a minority of functionless property-owners. The issue is vital, not only for them, but for the whole cause of Labour. Amid misrepresentation and calumny the miners are hewing a road along which other workers can march in the future.

Nor is it only for the sake of the mine-workers that the public ownership and democratic administration of the Coal Industry are indispensable. It is at least as necessary for the sake of the consumer of coal, on whom the burden of the present disorganization rests. In the last six months every interest which sees its power or its profits menaced by public ownership has sought once again to exploit the ancient strategy of pitting producers against consumers, and has warned the public in solemn accents that only the mine-owners stand between it and the Miners' Federation. They do, indeed. They stand between them so effectively that they intercepted in five years £160,000,000. That version of the confidence trick is an old one, and by this time is stale. In reality, it is only by hastening the transition to an organization of industry under which the miners will serve the public direct, without making profits for shareholders by way of payment for permission to do so, that the consumer will find a way out of his present sufferings.

For the truth is that, as far as the coal industry is concerned —and the coal industry does not stand alone—the industrial autocracy which has governed hitherto has broken down. The discipline upon which it relied to secure efficiency depended, in the last resort, upon the ability of the management to enforce its will by the threat of dismissal, which meant, in effect, by an appeal to hunger and fear. Always barbarous and inhuman, that discipline can be enforced today no longer, because the psychological conditions which made it possible have disappeared. Men will no longer give their labour and risk their lives for a system which they regard as morally indefensible and professionally incompetent. The alternative to it is the discipline of professional pride and responsibility —that the mine-workers should be recognized as partners in a communal enterprise, and have the power to discharge the obligations which that position will entail.

It is such a change, and only such a change, which will extricate the industry from the *impasse* into which it has been brought. For grave as are the technical deficiencies of the present organization which are criticized by the experts, it is not in these that the centre of the problem is to be found. The single greatest economic loss to the coal industry, and indeed to British industry as a whole, is the dissatisfaction which pervades the majority of those engaged in it; and if it is important to increase the output of wealth, it is not a paradox, but the statement of an elementary economic fact, to say that a change which made possible cordial and constructive co-operation on the part of the workers, would do more to produce that result than the discovery of a new coal-field or a generation of scientific invention. That co-operation will not be available in order to swell the dividends of shareholders. It will be forthcoming only if the coal industry is turned into an honourable public service, which is carried on for the benefit, not of a class, but of the whole community, and for the success of which the workers themselves bear, in conjunction with the representatives of the consumers, an effective and increasing responsibility.

IO

SOCIAL DEMOCRACY IN BRITAIN[1]

I

It is possible to conceive an economic system and social order which, while not immune to shocks from without, are normally regarded by those living under them with an approval so whole-hearted as to make the discussion of alternatives to them the mere pastime of an idle hour. Whether the complex of legal institutions, economic interests and psychological habits conventionally, if often misleadingly, epitomized as capitalism, enjoys that position in the United States, it is not for a foreigner to discuss. In Europe they held it once, but now hold it no longer. Great Britain, which played a not negligible part as their prophet and pioneer, is not an exception to that statement.

The term 'capitalism' is, of course, a highly ambiguous one. It is the description of a large genus with a variety of different species. Its connotation differs in the same country at different times, and in different countries at the same time. It may be highly individualistic or prolific in complexities of corporate organization; ruthlessly competitive, or with a leaning towards monopoly; determined to hold public authority at arm's length, or disposed, when occasion differs, to court it as an ally and use it as an instrument. It may even unite characteristics which, to the eye of uninstructed innocence, appear incompatible, by combining a vociferous enthusiasm for the blessings of free enterprise with a tenacious insistence on tariffs expressly designed to avert the risk that those blessings may be inflicted on it.

To ignore such diversities would obviously be naive: but one who considers the changes of the last two generations can hardly fail to be struck by one feature. It is the surprising

---

[1] Chapter in *The Christian Demand for Social Justice*, symposium by various writers. Edited by Bishop William Scarlett, New American Library, New York, 1949. The paper was intended for American readers.

reversal of attitudes that has taken place in that period towards an economic system which—whatever its most appropriate designation—as recently as the beginning of the present century, appeared unassailable. In parts of the Continent, notably in Eastern Europe, the Industrial Revolution was a thing of yesterday, and came, when it did, less through the gradual growth to maturity of native germs than as an alien importation. In those regions, therefore, the roots of the social order created by it lay near the surface, and a short way could be taken with them. Elsewhere, in Western Europe, and, particularly in England, where three centuries of history lie behind it, that order is so inextricably intertwined with individual psychologies and collective life that mere excision, even were that desired, would be out of the question. There, too, it has felt the encroachments of a rising tide, but the effect of the forces playing on it has not been catastrophic. It has been a gradual process of erosion—erosion of economic prestige, of political leadership, of moral authority—accompanied, since mankind cannot live on mere negations, by constructive counter-movements of thought and organization, which have gathered to themselves the loyalties and hopes that the old régime has lost the power to inspire.

The reasons for the crumbling of a once venerated idol must not now detain us; but institutions rest on psychological foundations, and to underestimate the consequences of this unanticipated conversion would be less than realistic. It means that the task of reconstruction, both for England and for several of her continental neighbours, is more subtle and exacting than the mere reparation of a shattered edifice. The revolt against capitalism has its source, not merely in material miseries, but in resentment against an economic system which dehumanizes existence by treating the mass of mankind, not as responsible partners in the co-operative enterprise of subduing nature to the service of man, but as instruments to be manipulated for the pecuniary advantage of a minority of property-owners, who themselves, in proportion as their aims are achieved, are too often degraded by the attainment of them.

The problem now confronting us must be approached on that plane. It is moral, and political, even more than economic.

It is a question, not only of the failures of the existing order, but of its standards of success. It is not merely to restore the conditions of material prosperity, urgent though such a restoration is. It is to work out a new social synthesis which may do justice both to the values of the Liberal era and to equally important aspects of life, to which that era, for all its virtues, was too often blind. It is to provide more compelling motives for the sustained co-operative effort which, under modern conditions of mass organization, civilization demands, by relating it to common purposes of a kind of appeal, not only to the interests, but to the conscience and reason, of all men of good will.

That task is to be approached by more than one path. It would be a very superficial view of the ferment now at work in Europe, which failed to trace its influence in literature, art, education and religious thought, as well as in the dusty world of politics. But politics have their place; and, as far as they are concerned, the historical form assumed by the struggle to create a more human social order is represented by one type or another of socialist movement. Socialism, however, is obviously a word with more than one meaning. As always in the case of political systems, its character varies with the practical realities, political, cultural and economic, of the specific environment in which it develops, and it is unprofitable to discuss it in general terms without defining the particular type of it which is under consideration.

The British variety has no claim to be unique. The Social Democratic genus, of which it is one species, is attacked, of course, from two different angles. It is denounced simultaneously both for the nauseous hypocrisy which causes it to betray its economic objectives for the sake of preserving the sterile formalities of political democracy, and for the reckless intransigence with which it imperils democracy by insisting on an economic reconstruction, which, in so far as it is realized, must inevitably, it is alleged, result in undermining it. The question of principle suggested by these contradictory indictments cannot here be discussed; but two observations are, perhaps in place.

The only sound test, in the first place, of a political system, is its practical effect on the lives of human beings. The war should have taught us one lesson, if it has taught us nothing more. It is idle for a nation to blazon Liberty, Equality, and Fraternity, or other resounding affirmations, on the façades of its public buildings, if to display the same motto in its factories and mines would arouse only the cynical laughter that greets a reminder of idealisms turned sour and hopes unfulfilled. What men demand is not merely paragraphs in constitutions, but results, in the form of arrangements which secure them the essentials of a civilized existence and show a proper respect for their dignity as human beings. Democracy must prove, if it is to survive, its faith by its works. It is unstable as a political system, as long as it remains a political system and little more, instead of producing, as it should, its own type of society and a manner of life in harmony with that type.

It is such a society and such a way of life that British socialists and their continental colleagues are labouring to create. They intend to create them, in the second place, not by jettisoning democratic institutions, but by using more assiduously the powers they confer. In the London of the 1930s, when Bloomsbury had just awoken to the recondite fact of the existence of a class struggle, and announced the discovery with bloodcurdling bleats, there were not wanting prophets who cried and cut themselves with knives at the alleged futility of political democracy. The rank and file of the Labour Movement were then, and remain now, unmoved by these antics. They know the effects of the paralysis and perversions, to which, in the absence of a vigorous public opinion, democracy is subject, a good deal more intimately than the melodious intellectuals who harrow refined audiences with tearful cries of stinking fish; but they know also what they have gained from it. They regard democracy, not as an obstacle to socialism, but as an instrument for attaining it, and socialism, not as the antithesis of democracy, but as the extension of democratic principles into spheres of life which previously escaped their influence. Given the acceptance of that view, controversies may be bitter; but, once a political system has been put on a popular basis, the conflict takes place within the limits fixed by it. It turns, not on the merits or demerits of that system itself, but on the specific purposes for which, from time to time, opposing parties seek to use it.

Since Great Britain is a democratic country, it is on these lines that the struggle to extend socialism and to resist is today being fought out. Her traditional political and civil liberties are, to speak with moderation, not less secure under her Socialist Government than they were under its predecessors. The new feature in the situation is the effort to add economic justice to them. To one acquainted with British conditions the standpoint from which that task is approached should cause no surprise. The Labour Party rejoices, of course, in the possession of the lunatic fringe which is a necessary ingredient in any movement aspiring to be representative. But the bulk of the sober and experienced persons who, after years spent in governing great cities, or administering trade unions, or practising law, medicine and other professions, or running their businesses, enter the House of Commons as Labour members are not of the kind which succumbs readily either to apocalyptic illusions or to the worship of power-politics.

Few of them would deny that capitalism—if that convenient shorthand may be used—has played an indispensable part in releasing imprisoned energies, and mobilizing them, with profit as the magnet, for the production of wealth; or that a social order of a different kind must be built on the technological foundations laid by it; or that, in a world, outside a few favoured regions, still miserably poor, an increase in the output of wealth is of urgent importance. All of them however, while paying a respectful tribute to these venerable platitudes, would find in them a reason, not for repudiating their socialist objective, but for the more strenuous pursuit of it. It is needless, they would say, to labour the commonplace that the grand achievement of the last century has been the conquest of nature and the increase of material wealth resulting from it. That truism is self-evident, and no instructed socialist disputes it. The question of immediate moment is on another plane. It is whether man's capacity for the rational management of his communal affairs has kept pace with his mastery of natural forces, and whether, as a consequence, the powerful productive engine which he now commands is employed to the best advantage in the interest of all.

That question is one to be answered in terms, not of economics or technology alone—though both have their place—but of human psychology and social organization. Ordinary men desire a reasonable measure of security against unmerited misfortunes, caused by forces which, as individuals, they are powerless to control. Do statistics of the fluctuations of employment during the past thirty years—does, for example, the American crisis of 1929–34—suggest that that not extravagant demand is fully met? Without yearning for a pedantic uniformity of circumstance or income, they are sufficiently social-minded to regard gross and arbitrary inequalities, which pamper some, pinch others, and degrade both, as inhuman and nauseating. Do the figures of the distribution of wealth indicate that, before the war, these uncivilized disparities were wholly avoided? They are attached to the doctrine expressed in the venerable phrase that 'what touches all should be approved by all'. Do the well-known facts as to the concentration of ownership, and still more of control, encourage a belief that matters of economic strategy, on which the welfare of whole populations depends, are decided, not by the agents of a minority of property-owners, but by bodies responsible to the public whom industry exists to serve?

British socialists find it difficult to answer such questions in the affirmative. Not only so, but they think that, while a social order marked by these morbid phenomena may well have been a stage of unavoidable barbarism through which industrial societies had to pass on their journey towards civilization, it is folly to cling to it, once the necessity for it has passed. Granted, in short, the past services rendered by capitalism, the time has come, it seems to them, when we can at least do better. That being so, it is our duty, they hold, to mobilize the resources of knowledge and public spirit required to enable us to take the next step forward.

That conclusion, if accepted, imposes onerous obligations. The modification of the complex structure of social organization, which is the aim of socialists, is an arduous business. It demands, not mere demolition, but construction; and constructive policies do not come either by providential inspiration or by a simple inspection of the evils to be cured. They emerge, if at all, only as the result of years of dull drudgery devoted to the investigation of specific problems; the formulation, rejection and re-formulation of provisional solutions; and finally, if fortune favours, the discovery of a line of action which will at once meet the case, stand expert criticism, and be capable of application, not in some imaginary Utopia, but in the rough-and-tumble of an imperfect world. What, in short, a Socialist Government can do, when in office, depends largely on the trouble taken to mature its plans before its advent to power gives it a chance of acting on them.

Such preparatory work is not always possible, and can never be adequate; but by the time when, in 1918, a reconstructed Labour Party started on the second lap in its history, a version of socialism had been hammered out of a kind not too sublime to be turned into the prosaic sections, sub-sections and schedules of Acts of Parliament. It included the legal enforcement of minimum standards of life and work; the expansion of different forms of communal provision designed to make accessible to all advantages previously confined to the minority with the means to buy them; the use of financial measures to reduce economic inequalities; and the transference of certain foundation services to public ownership.

But in a changing world no programme can pretend to finality. The inter-war period brought its own crop of problems, and the search for solutions to them added new ingredients. Unemployment in two forms—the chronic misery seen at its worst in the so-called 'special' areas, which was represented by an unemployment averaging fourteen per cent for eighteen years on end, and the shock of the great depression—was a nightmare. Two economists, both politically Liberals, produced policies which, in their advocacy of action by the State to maintain full employment, were important contributions to socialist thought. Naturally, the Labour Party borrowed from them.

By the thirties it had become apparent that, while the newer industries were doing well, the condition of some of the older, such as coal and cotton, which had in the past been the backbone of British economic life, was anything but healthy. In such circumstances, the optimistic assumption that productive efficiency would look after itself, and that socialists could confine their attention to ensuring that its fruits were fairly shared, was obviously out of date. If the ostensible leaders of the industries in question were incapable of modernizing them, then a Socialist Government, when it came to power, must do the job itself, or see that it was done. Monopolistic practices were not a novel feature of the economic system; but, in the proportions that they then showed signs of assuming, they unquestionably were. In view of their effect on productivity, prices, and employment, no responsible Government could ignore them.

The combined influence of these three factors prepared the way for the emergence of a fourth. Planning is among the most ambiguous of categories; but, even before the war and post-war shortages made the deliberate economizing of man-power and materials a matter of necessity, it was permissible to doubt whether, in the light of recent experience, an undis-criminating reliance on the free play of economic self-interest would continue in future to be so adequate a formula as it had appeared in the past.

As far, therefore, as domestic matters were concerned, the programme on which the Labour Party fought the last (1945) election contained little that was novel. It was not an improvisa-tion, but an epitome of prescriptions, some of which, if in diluted doses, had already been tried with good results and most of which had been made familiar by prolonged discussion.

II

The principal new departures initiated by the Labour Govern-ment may conveniently be classified under three main heads. The first has been concerned with the extension and improve-ment of the various forms of communal provision—education, public health, insurance against sickness and unemployment, old age and widows' pensions, medical care and school-meals for children—which, though widely differing both in their purposes and their effects, are in England illogically grouped together under the un-illuminating name of the Social Services. Mainly under Conservative ministries, they had undergone, in the inter-war period, a development which, when allowance is made for the change in the price-level, had more than doubled the expenditure on them. The necessity both for their further enlargement and for their systematization had become by 1939 common ground between parties.

145

The (war-time) Coalition Government had taken some steps in that direction. It had been responsible in 1944 for a new Education Act, and, in the following year, for a Family Allowance Act. Of the latter something is said below; the former prepared the way for the most far-reaching reconstruction carried out since a public system of education was first brought into existence. It affects every side of that system, from Nursery schools or classes to the education of adults; but its most significant innovations were, perhaps, four. It substituted a universal system of secondary education for the selective arrangements which had hitherto existed. It fixed fifteen, instead of fourteen, as the minimum age for the cessation of compulsory education, with the addition that, as soon as circumstances allowed, attendance should be legally obligatory to sixteen. It abolished fees, and made secondary education free, in all but a small minority of secondary schools. It provided for the creation of a system of compulsory part-time continuation schools to follow full-time education up to the age of eighteen. Henceforward, therefore, all children, and not merely,. as hitherto, a minority, will pass, between eleven and twelve, to one type or another of secondary school, and the disastrous gap between the school and industry will be partially bridged by continued education.

Though piloted through Parliament by an enlightened Conservative minister, the measure owed not a little, it is fair to say, to the Labour Party, which has long given 'secondary education for all' a prominent place in its programme. The duty both of enforcing the new minimum leaving age, in the teeth of short-sighted clamour that the shortage of workers made the reform inopportune, and also of bringing into operation other parts of the Act—in view of the shortage of materials for building schools no easy task—has devolved on the Labour Government. It had been decided before the conclusion of the war that the provision for university education required to be greatly expanded; and it was the first Labour Chancellor of the Exchequer who took the important step of enlarging and redefining the powers and duties of the body— the University Grants Committee—on whose advice the State's financial aid to the universities is given. The present Government's chief contributions to the Social Services have been made, however, in a different field. They consist of its Social Security and Health measures.

A system of pooling risks by unemployment and sickness insurance had been established in England before the First World War. Repeatedly extended in the next quarter of a century, it suffered, when the Labour Government came to power, from the gaps and inconsistencies to be expected after a long series of piecemeal modifications. The details of the new structure are necessarily complicated; but its larger outlines can be simply stated. In the first place, a comprehensive National Insurance Act has consolidated the former Health and Unemployment Insurance schemes; has placed them under a single Ministry of National Insurance; and has established a universal system, with standard contributions and benefits—both, but especially the latter, substantially increased—under which every citizen is insured against sickness and unemployment from the age at which compulsory education ceases to that at which he or she qualifies for a retiring pension, special provision being made for the needs of maternity, in the shape of a grant on confinement and allowances, up to thirteen weeks, in the case of mothers normally in employment, as well as for widows and orphans. In the second place, a further Act provides for the special case of injury or disease incurred by workers in the course of their employment. Henceforward, the injured worker, instead of being required to make good a claim, often stubbornly contested, to compensation under the Workmen's Compensation Acts, will receive as a matter of course, subject to periodical medical reports on his condition, industrial injuries benefit up to six months, and subsequently, if he suffers from permanent disablement, a disablement pension graded according to the degree of his incapacity.

The third piece of legislation, the National Health Act, is intended to make the best medical treatment available for the whole population, irrespective of the financial means of different families. It does not, as has been suggested, 'nationalize medicine'; and the medical profession, which at first looked askance at the measure as threatening the independence of the private practitioner, decided, after some hesitation, to co-operate in making a success of it. It establishes a service free for all at the time of treatment, the cost of which will be met partly from insurance contributions, partly from local rates and partly from grants from the National Exchequer. Hospitals are transferred from the hands of Local Authorities and voluntary bodies—the latter often short of funds—to the Ministry of Health, under which they will be administered by Regional Boards, composed, to the extent of one-half, of medical practitioners, and, for the other half, of nominees of the Ministry and the Local Health Authorities. Doctors are at liberty to continue their private practices, or to enter the national service, or to combine the two, as they themselves decide. Provision is made for a wide development, as soon as circumstances allow, of Health Centres, equipped and maintained from public funds, where, when they so choose, they will engage in group practice.

Finally, a principle not previously accepted in England has been embodied in an act already mentioned, the credit for which belongs to the Coalition Government. It is common knowledge that the period of maximum strain in a family occurs when several children have been born, and the eldest is not yet of an age to earn. The Family Allowance Act of 1945 is designed to meet that situation. It does so partly by establishing allowances in the shape of a small cash payment for each child after the first, up either to the age when compulsory education ceases or to that of sixteen, whichever is the highest, partly by provision in kind, such as milk, vitamins, and cod-liver oil for expectant mothers and during the first year of a child's life, together with special supplies of the first for children of school age, and meals in public primary and secondary schools. Visitors to England periodically complain that milk is short. In reality, the average consumption per head is considerably higher than at any previous period. It is true, however, that, since a larger proportion of the supply than before 1939 goes to those, in particular children, who need it most, there is less for adults—other than invalids—who can contrive, without intolerable hardship, to moderate their appetite for it. It is a question whether that minute concession to Christian ethics can appropriately be regarded as an occasion for tears.

It is possible, by means of a wisely planned system of communal provision, to ensure that the whole population enjoys, as far as environmental influences are concerned, equal opportunities of health and education, and is equally protected against the contingencies of life. Such a system, therefore, is not an excrescence upon socialist policy, but an essential part of it. It is an investment in the development of human energies, which will, in time, pay handsome dividends; and it was proper that a high place should be given by a Labour Government to the effort to create it.

The second and third main departments of that Government's policy are on a different plane. They are concerned, not with sharing more equitably the wealth produced, but with organizing more effectively the energies which produce it. They include anti-unemployment measures; the nationalization of certain important services; and action to eliminate avoidable causes of inefficiency in the case of industries—which will for long remain the great majority—not yet promoted to the dignity of public ownership.

The steps taken under the first head may, at the moment, appear otiose. In order, however, to produce their effect, expedients to avert unemployment must be prepared in advance, at a time when, as today, the problem is the shortage, not of jobs, but of workers to fill them. The Labour Party does not share the belief, expressed by eminent persons in the United States shortly before the catastrophe of 1929, that the level of productive activity can safely be left to take care of itself, nor does it take the view once fashionable both in that country and Great Britain, that decisions based on the self-interest—enlightened or otherwise—of entrepreneurs and investors should be the chief factor determining it. On the contrary, it regards the economic waste and social misery caused by recurrent unemployment as a scandal to our civilization, and holds that to take every possible step to prevent it is among the first duties of Governments. Thanks largely to the work of economic thinkers, such as Keynes and Beveridge, the partial, though doubtless not the complete, suppression of an evil till recently accepted, like typhus and cholera a century and a half ago, as though it were an Act of God, not the result of human folly and greed, no longers appears to be beyond the wit of man. Naturally, therefore, measures to avert its future recurrence were among the earliest preoccupations of the present British Cabinet.

In this matter the Labour Party makes no pretence to the possession of an infallible formula. It has merely sought the best advice available, and attempted to act on it. Given a planning organization, to act as an economic general staff, the nucleus of which was created during the war, and which has now, with the necessary modifications, been placed under the Chancellor of the Exchequer, the first necessity was for the Government to be invested with adequate powers of control over the financial system. The principal means employed for that purpose have been three. The Bank of England has at last been added to the not inconsiderable number of Central Banks in public ownership, and its power to issue directions to other banks has been increased. The war-time control of new capital issues by means of a licensing system has been continued, and the Treasury has been empowered to guarantee loans for the reconstruction or development of any industry up to a maximum of £50,000,000, a figure which can, with parliamentary sanction, be increased. A National Investment Council has been established, to 'advise and assist the Government in so organizing, and, when necessary, stimulating, investment as to promote full employment'. Henceforward, therefore, the main levers of short and long term credit will be in public hands, and it will be possible for both to be managed with a single eye to the public interest. Both a blunder, such as that of 1925, when, in deference to City sentiment, the export industries were sacrificed by the return to gold at too high a parity, and the recurrent imbecility of pouring capital into luxury flats, picture-houses and other investments which chance to hit the public fancy, at a time when coal and cotton were starved of the resources required to reconstruct them, are less likely to be repeated.

Nor do measures of this order stand alone. Budgetary policy has an obvious bearing on the level of employment; and that favoured by Labour opinion has its contribution to make. Some twenty years have elapsed since it was remarked by a Royal Commission of unimpeachable propriety, presided over by a banker who was a pillar of respectability, that the social services, since they are not subject to sharp fluctuations, are a stabilizing factor in the national economy; while it was the most eminent of modern British economists who wrote that 'in contemporary conditions, the growth of wealth, so far from being dependent on the abstinence of the rich, is much more likely to be impeded by it'. In combining an expansion of communal provision with a steeper graduation of taxation, the Government has complied with these prescriptions.

A further, and more important, influence on the side of increased stability is likely to be exercised by a third element in its policy. It is now generally agreed that fluctuations in investment have played a major part in producing alternations of boom and depression, and that those alternations are seen at their sharpest in the producer-goods industries. That public investment, which can be deliberately regulated from year to year, is likely, given a reasonable measure of prevision, to fluctuate less violently than that of private individuals and corporations is equally a truism. The larger, in short, the sector of the national economy in which investment can be made with some approximation to a settled plan, the greater the State's command of the means to neutralize the grave evils caused by the anarchic oscillations of private industry.

Since 1945, the sector has been in process of expansion. The housing programme, under which, in the three years following the conclusion of the war, accommodation was provided for not far short of a million and a half persons; the town and country planning policy; the Distribution of Industries Act; and the development areas established under it, are cases in point. The transference, apart from the special case of the Bank of England, of half a dozen industries to public ownership, though primarily prompted by other considerations, is, in this connection also, not without its advantages. In considering the reasons for the adoption of a policy which, though not new in principle, is novel on the present scale, certain commonplaces are, perhaps, in order. The line, in the first place, between the area of economic life resigned to the activities of profit-making entrepreneurs and that administered by public authorities, has never possessed the fixity often ignorantly ascribed to it. In reality, as a glance at the history of Europe is sufficient to show, it has been repeatedly re-drawn; and an observer of that impressive socialist undertaking, the TVA, may be pardoned for feeling some uncertainty whether even the most virtuous of people is an exception to that statement.

Prima facie, there is nothing surprising in the view that, as circumstances change, a reclassification of the spheres of private and public undertakings is periodically required. Whether in any particular instance, it is desirable or not is a question to be decided in the light, not of resounding affirmations of the virtues either of free enterprise or of socialization, but of the facts of the case.

It is an illusion, to suppose, in the second place, that the advocacy of an extension of public ownership is either confined in England to members of one party or advanced by that party as a formula of universal application. Authorities whose political sympathies, if classifiable at all, are not to be grouped under any single heading, have recommended it, on grounds of practical expediency, in the case of monopolies—a large category—agricultural land, transport, coal and power. The Labour Party approaches the problem in an equally realistic spirit. It is true, of course, that great aggregations of economic power in private hands are open to objection on moral and political grounds, as a menace to democracy and freedom, and that Labour, which is rightly sensitive to their deleterious influence on the quality of civic life, looks to the extension of public ownership as one expedient, though only one, for averting that danger. Practical realities, however, determine that its policy in this field, as in others, shall not be wholesale and indiscriminate, but shall advance step by step, as a case for it is established. The result has been a process of selective nationalization, undertaken when, on one or more of several different grounds, the balance of advantages favours that course.

In the case of the industries hitherto nationalized, such grounds have not been far to seek. Partly, it is to be presumed, for that reason, opposition to this aspect of the Government's policy has been less vocal that might have been expected. The transfer to public ownership of civil aviation and of long-distance communications by cable and wireless passed almost unnoticed. The nationalization of gas and electricity, if challenged in the House of Commons, stirred outside it only minor ripples. The more formidable task of converting into a unified service the railways, long-distance road haulage, and some sixty canal undertakings, together with subsidiaries such as the docks and harbours owned by bodies of several kinds, naturally aroused more anxiety; but, here again, objections had as their target less the principle of public ownership than specific questions relating to the structure and organization of the new system. Just under thirty years ago, the recommendation that the mines should be nationalized, which was advanced by the majority of the Coal Commission presided over by the late Lord Sankey, aroused a storm of opposition. When, in 1946, that proposal became at last an Act of Parliament, not a dog barked.

The transfer of property in return for compensation, which nationalization involves, is a means, not an end. Its purpose is to ensure that services, on which the general welfare depends, shall be conducted with a single eye to that objective, under authorities accountable for their proceedings to the public. Its success depends, therefore, not on the mere change of ownership, but on the degree to which advantage is taken of the opportunity offered by it to secure first-class management, to carry through measures of reorganization which private enterprise was unable or unwilling to undertake, and to enlist the active co-operation of employees in increasing production. It is to be judged by its practical results on consumers, on workers and on the national prosperity; and, though the long decline in output, which went on in the coal industry under private ownership, has been replaced since nationalization by a slow upward movement, a longer period must elapse before a confident pronouncement on results can be made.

Even, however, when this part of the programme of the present parliament has been carried to completion, some four-fifths of the industrial personnel of the country will continue to be employed in industries in private hands; and, while some of the latter are not open to serious criticism on the score of inefficiency, there are others whose condition leaves not a little to be desired. Policy here has followed several lines. The first step taken has been to throw on the industries in question the responsibility for preparing such plans for improvement as may be needed, by appointing 'working parties' composed of employers and trade unionists to submit reports on the subject to the Board of Trade. In the second place, the Government has taken powers, under the Industrial Organization Act of 1947, to set up Development Councils to bring approved

schemes of reorganization into operation, and, in certain cases
—for example that of the cotton industry, in which Parliament
has empowered it to pay grants up to twenty-five per cent of
the cost of re-equipment—has stimulated modernization by
financial assistance. Third, it has carried a Monopolies and
Restrictive Practices Act, under which a Commission acting
under the Board of Trade will inquire into such practices, and
a competent Minister will have power, subject to affirmative
resolutions in Parliament, to make orders prohibiting such of
them as are found to be contrary to the public interest. Finally,
and not least important, it has taken steps to ensure that the
reproach of a neglect of the economic applications of science,
which, though not generally true, had, in certain old-fashioned
industries, too much validity, shall become a thing of the past.
It has arranged for the supply of university-trained scientists
to be largely increased; has made funds available to promote
research, not only in technology, but in the economic and
social sciences; has encouraged the establishment of an Institute of Industrial Management, partly financed from public
funds, to conduct investigations into the problems of management, and has expanded the activities of the public Production
Efficiency Service, whose advice is available for all firms
desiring it.

III

In the immense lottery of war, sacrifices neither are nor can
be equally shared. The economic embarrassments inherited
by Great Britain from a conflict in which she fought, like her
principal antagonist, from the first day to the last, and was not
careful, in contributing to the common cause, to consider her
own future, have not been a trifle. Of the measures by which
she is grappling with these inevitable difficulties, and will in
due course overcome them, this is not the place to speak. Nor
has the time yet come when the larger policies of her Government can be judged by results. Their tendency is, however,
obvious. It will be interrupted by recurrent checks and throw-
backs. Since, however, the force behind it is not merely a
political party, but the set of British life, it will not be arrested.
Like earlier movements in her history, which also wound their

way amid shoals and sand-banks, it will produce, in due course, its distinctive social order.

If present indications may be trusted, that order will be found, as it develops, to differ not less from the capitalist plutocracies formerly predominant in Western Europe than from the Eastern dictatorships. Some of its characteristics, if only in embryo, can already be discerned. Parliamentary Government and personal liberty not only continue in England unimpaired, but derive a heightened significance both from the successful employment of the former to effect by consent changes elsewhere imposed by violence, and from the more positive content acquired by the latter as the result of the firmer guarantees for opportunity, economic security and social well-being now added to it. Private interests count for less as a determinant of economic strategy, and public interests for more. The preponderance which, in the fluctuating balance of power between property and creative work, formerly belonged to ownership is now passing to Labour. Social solidarity has been strengthened as the essentials of civilization, once the privilege of a minority, have increasingly become a common possession. Judged by the distribution of income, a more equalitarian society than existed in pre-war England, and than exists today in the Soviet Union or in the United States, is in process of creation. The maxim borrowed by Matthew Arnold from Menander—'Choose equality and shun greed'—is, doubtless, a far from all-sufficient formula. In a world, however, where Communist social theory and American economic practice agree in repudiating it, it is not perhaps a misfortune that one more people has been added to the small number of those disposed to take it seriously.

All social organisms secrete their own toxins: and, when one of them succumbs to the conviction of immunity, that illusion itself is a symptom of disease. Social Democracy, as its more sensible adherents are aware, is no exception to that statement. Only a simpleton supposes that a change of organization is a prophylactic against the imbecilities of human nature; and it has long been a commonplace that the socialization of a service, whether coal or education, is important, not as the end of the process of reforming it, but as enabling that process to be effectively begun. It is true, no doubt, that there were features of the pre-war economic system from which even a partially socialized society may not unreasonably be expected to be free. The reckless plundering of nature; the orgies of financial immorality which disgraced the early railway age in Great Britain and America, and of which less heroic examples still occasionally recur; the dissipation of resources in superfluous, futile, or even mischievous, ventures to the prejudice of objects of urgent importance; the callous exploitation of human energies, with its inevitable concomitants of tyranny and violence—gross and scandalous offences of this order are not likely to be repeated by it.

The fact remains, nevertheless, that such a society will be faced with problems of its own, and will, doubtless, like its capitalist predecessors, commit its own blunders in solving them. It may be tempted, in developing its social services, to pander to popular tastes, instead of instructing them, and to devote an excessive proportion of its annual income to needs pressed on it by a mass demand, to the neglect of less clamorous, but, on a long view, more important, requirements. Errors will occur in the selection of services to be transferred to public ownership. Unsuitable forms of organization will be tried, modified and discarded. The procedure to be followed in selecting and training management; the most effective methods, not merely of ensuring professional competence, but of encouraging a high standard of initiative and audacity; the technique of combining public control over the larger issues of economic strategy with a free hand for officers in the choice of tactical means, will not at once be discovered. The evil legacy of suspicion left by capitalism among the rank and file of workers cannot, unfortunately, be wound up by the sections of an Act of Parliament. It may well be the case that a generation must elapse before a cordial partnership between the public bodies responsible for the conduct of a nationalized industry and the employees in them, of a character to ensure that the latter make, through their organizations, their full contribution to the efficiency of the service, can successfuly be established.

In matters of this kind socialists, no more than their critics, can pretend to the possession of an infallible formula. The proper attitude for them is obvious. It is to keep an open mind; to decline to relapse into the complacent dogmatism too often found among the paladins of the 'free enterprise system'; to learn from experience; to be candid in admitting mistakes and prompt in correcting them. While, however, topics of this practical order were never more keenly discussed in Great Britain than they are today, the most significant feature of recent controversy is different. It is the emergence, behind these problems of technique and method, of a conflict of opinion on more fundamental issues. After two generations of debate on socialism there is now taking place, on both sides of the argument, an instructive change of emphasis. Increasingly immersed in the tasks of government, local and national, socialists have exchanged the prophetic rôle of the past for the habits and mentality of the practical administrator. Their opponents have moved in the opposite direction. The former have become realists, sometimes even to excess. The latter, while continuing to challenge specific aspects of their policy, no longer deride them as economic innocents or hare-brained Utopians, but invoke against them the majestic imponderables of religion and morality.

Partly through the growth of giant corporations administered by corps of salaried officials; partly as a result of the growth of quasi-monopolies, in which the spur of competition, if not wholly absent, is blunted; partly because one result of two wars, as well as of domestic policies pursued by all parties, has been an impressive increase in the supply of economic talent in the public service, less is heard than formerly of the impracticability of socialism and of the disasters to be expected from bureaucratic incompetence. More is said of the menace thought to be offered by it to the higher interests of the nation. The enlargement of the economic functions of public authorities may result, it is conceded, in a more effective utilization of the nation's resources, and a more equitable distribution of the produce of co-operative effort; but the debit side of the account will not, it is argued, be a trifle. The State, as its grasp extends, will make a desert, and call it efficiency. It will jeopardize the moral values—liberty, disinterested cultural activities, the intimacies and informalities of human intercourse—of which economic arrangements, however admirable, are no more than the squalid scaffolding.

Thus the wheel has come full circle. The apologist for

capitalism, without ceasing to laud the material benefits conferred by it, asks, with tremulous apprehension, 'What shall it profit a society, if it gain the whole world and lose its soul?' The socialist, accustomed in his credulous youth to be ridiculed as a visionary idealist with his head in the clouds, finds himself denounced with equal unction in his degraded old age as a sordid materialist with his eyes glued to the cash-register.

Economic efficiency is important as a condition of vitality, individual and collective, but is otherwise without significance. Socialists, who preached wisdom in the street when no man regarded it, should welcome, as belated stirrings of the spirit, the tributes to that truism now paid by their opponents. Nor when, as commonly in America, an indifference to freedom is the burden of the ethical indictment brought against them, need they look far for an answer.

It is obvious, in the first place, that the suggestion of affinities between Social Democracy and Communism, advanced by uninstructed critics to lend colour to that charge, rests, as the relations between the two unfortunately show, on a naïf misconception of the characteristics of both. Whatever the case for Totalitarianism, it is of its essence that, since only a single party is, in practice, tolerated, no peaceful procedure exists for the periodical supersession of one set of rulers by another. In such circumstances, the crucial distinction between sovereignty and mere power is absent or blurred; and opposition to the Government is readily confounded, when convenient to the latter, with treason to the State. Civil liberty, therefore, as experience shows, is necessarily insecure. Political liberty, of which the right of a majority to make and unmake Governments, and of individuals to speak, write and agitate with that end in view, is an indispensable part, is non-existent.

Only ignorance or prejudice would deny the technical and economic achievements of the Soviet Union; but dams, bridges, power-plants and steel-works, however admirable, are not a substitute for human rights; and the contrast between Russian Police Collectivism and the socialism of Western Europe is too obvious to need emphasis. The former has behind it a tradition of autocracy unbroken for four centuries; the later the aspirations of people whose account with absolutist pretensions has long been settled, and who regard with a sceptical eye the doctrine that the one infallible specific for social emancipation is surrender to a dictatorship. All of them have drunk, with the usual recurrent starts of animal aversion, of the Christian conception of the dignity of man. All of them, while repudiating the arid provincialisms of the Manchester School, have been profoundly affected by the ecumenical liberalism which proclaimed as the goal of political effort the free development of human personality, unimpeded by privileges of class, capricious inequalities of circumstance, or arbitrary action by despotic rulers. The protection of minorities, tolerance for dissident opinions, the rule of law, the security of the individual against the Executive, the responsibility of Governments to popularly elected chambers, are characteristic of all of them.

The British version of socialism, therefore, has democracy as its basis. In labouring to add new economic storeys to the house, it has no intention of destroying its political foundations. Its attitude to freedom is no exception to that statement. It involves, not the curtailment of liberties, but their more general extension, and is, for that reason, denounced as tyrannical by those whose authority is likely, as a consequence, to suffer a diminution. Classes already at the top of the ladder may fall, but cannot rise. The construction which they put on freedom is the result of that position. Whether consciously or not, it is, in large measure, a defence mechanism. It is a doctrine of liberty which is disposed to regard it as involving, not action to enlarge opportunities and raise individual faculty to the highest possible level, but guarantees for the continued enjoyment by fortunate individuals and groups of such powers and advantages as past history and the present social order may happen to have conferred on them.

To the socialist, who considers the realities of existence among the undistinguished multitude of his fellow-citizens, that tranquil identification of liberty with the arrangements congenial to a favoured minority seems the sin against the Holy Ghost. He regards freedom, not primarily as a possession to be defended—though, when the occasion has arisen, he has known how to defend it—but as a goal to be achieved. He interprets it as implying the utmost possible development of the capacities of every human being, and the deliberate organization of society for the attainment of that objective.

It would be superfluous to add yet another catalogue of essential rights to the libraries of such lists which already exist; but two observations may be made on all of them. In the first place, if the rights are to be an effective guarantee of freedom, they must not be merely formal, like the right of all who can afford it to dine at the Ritz. They must be such that, whenever the occasion for their exercise arises, they can, in fact, be exercised. The rights to vote and combine, if not wholly valueless, are obviously attenuated, if the use of the former means eviction, and of the latter the sack; the right to the free choice of an occupation, if the preliminary expenses of professional training are prohibitive; the right of a man to give his best to his work, if the economic system condemns him to unemployment; the right to justice, if no poor man can pay for it; the right to 'life, liberty and the pursuit of happiness', if the environment is such as to ensure that a considerable proportion of those born will die within twelve months, and that the happiness-investments of the remainder are a gambling stock.

In the second place, the rights which are essential to freedom must secure the liberties of all, not merely of a minority. Some sage has remarked that marriage would not be regarded as a national institution if, while five per cent of the population were polygamous, the remainder completed their earthly pilgrimage unsolaced and unencumbered by husbands or wives. The same is true of freedom. A society in which some groups can do much what they please, while others can do little of what they ought, may have virtues of its own: but freedom is not one of them. It is free in so far, and only in so far, as all the elements composing it are able in fact, not merely in theory, to make the most of their powers, to grow to their full stature, to do what they conceive to be their duty, and—since liberty should not be too austere—to have their fling when they feel like it. In so far as the opportunity to lead a life worthy of human beings is confined to a minority, what is commonly called freedom would more properly be described as privilege.

As far, therefore, as matters of principle are concerned, the meaning of freedom is not obscure. The practical interpretation of principles in terms of policy and institutions raises problems of a different order. It varies, and properly varies, from age to age and people to people, with the varying conditions of different societies. There have been circumstances—those, for example, of a simple economic system combined with political absolutism—in which the chief enemy of freedom was the despotism of an autocrat, and the most immediately effective method enabling freedom to breathe was to exclude as many spheres of life as possible from governmental control. It is equally obvious, however, that, in the different conditions of an industrial civilization, the effect of that alluring formula is precisely the opposite.

It is still constantly assumed by privileged classes that, when the State holds its hand, what remains, as the result of its inaction, is liberty. In reality, as far as the mass of mankind is concerned, what commonly remains is, not liberty, but tyranny. In urban communities with dense populations, or in great productive undertakings employing armies of workers, someone must make rules and ensure that they are kept, or life becomes impossible and the wheels do not turn. If public power does not make them, the effect is not that every individual is free to make them for himself. It is that they are made by private power—by landlords interested in increasing rents or by capitalists interested in increasing profits. The result, in either case, is not freedom, but a dictatorship, which is not the less oppressive because largely unconscious, and because those whom it profits regard it, quite sincerely, as identical with liberty.

The classical example in the past was the condition of British wage-earners in the days when trade unions were still feeble, industrial codes crude, social services in their infancy, and measures either to prevent unemployment or to assist its victims to weather the storm not yet in existence. Nor, in that respect, has British experience been exceptional. Whether the black lists, yellow-dog contracts, company unions, spies, under-cover men, armed guards, gas-bombs, revolvers and machine-guns, and the rest of the American apparatus of coercion described in the report of the La Follette Committee of 1936, contributed greatly to the emancipation of the workers of the Land of Liberty, it would be presumptuous for a foreigner to inquire. As far as Europe is concerned, the lessons of history are clear. The increase in the freedom of ordinary men and women during the last two generations has taken place, not in spite of the action of Governments, but because of it. It has been due to the fact that, once political democracy had found its feet, popularly elected chambers began, under the pressure of their electors, to prescribe minimum standards of life and work, to extend public services, to pool surplus wealth and employ it for the common good, to confer a legal status on trade unions, and generally to treat their economically weaker citizens as human beings entitled to the opportunities, advantages, and security against unmerited misfortune, which had previously been confined to the economically strong. The mother of liberty has, in fact, been law.

That process was for long carried forward hesitatingly and with reluctance, by Governments which only half believed in it. Today, amid the jungle of adventitious obstacles left by the war, it is advancing in England rapidly and with conviction. It involves, of course, a substantial enlargement of the activities of public bodies; and it is here, in the debatable land between economics and politics, that the counter-attack is launched. The present writer, as his readers, doubtless, have discovered, does not, to his shame, study the works of economic theorists with the assiduity that they deserve, for the reason—if it is a reason and not mere weakness of the flesh—explained to her pupil by the school-mistress in that ancient, but admirable play, *The Importance of Being Ernest*: 'Do not read Mill's chapter on the fall of the rupee, my dear; it is too exciting for a young girl.' If his esteemed colleague, the author of *The Road to Serfdom*,[1] had confined himself to a forecast of the economic catastrophe threatened by socialism, he cannot say that, like the devils in Scripture, he would have believed and trembled; but he would certainly have trembled even while he disbelieved. Professor von Hayek has chosen as his target, however, not the economics of socialism, but the political and cultural nemesis which, he is convinced, it entails. His curtain falls on a world in which personal liberty, freedom of thought and speech, tolerance, objective science, private and public morality, have one by one, as socialism advances, been ruthlessly extinguished, and universal darkness covers all. It is,

[1] By F. A. Hayek (Routledge, London, 1944).

perhaps, not presumptuous, therefore, for one of the prospective serfs to hazard an opinion on the doom awaiting him.

The villain in Professor von Hayek's tragedy is, of course, the Planning and Organizing State. On his conception of planning it is needless to dwell, since it is not one which any British socialist of standing has ever accepted. Professor von Hayek, it would appear, understands by the term a comprehensive programme, embracing the whole range of economic activities, under which the quantity and quality of every article to be produced, from steel-plants to pins, and the occupation and payment of every individual, are prescribed in advance for a term of years by a central authority—an authority uninfluenced by the views of consumers or producers, acknowledging no responsibility, however indirect, to a representative assembly, and conducting its affairs by the issue of orders, the infringement of which is a criminal offence. Given these assumptions, it is not surprising that a Totalitarian monster should emerge as his conclusion, since he has been at pains to include Totalitarianism among his premises.

The version of planning expounded by him is, doubtless, a possible one, and his readers should be grateful to him for developing its implications. To imply, however, as Professor von Hayek appears to do, that the procedure whose horrifying consequences he portrays with such force alone needs to be considered, or that all other procedures must necessarily lead to the same fatal goal, is to beg all questions. If, as is commonly held by British socialists, the essential characteristic of a planned economy consists, not as Professor von Hayek seems to suggest, in a detailed budget of production, but in the transference for the responsibility for the higher ranges of economic strategy from profit-making entrepreneurs to a national authority, his mystery of iniquity is attenuated to a mare's nest and his bloodthirsty Leviathan becomes a serviceable drudge. It is not easy to specify what, if any, liberties would be jeopardized by the substitution of such an authority, pursuing, with full responsibility to the Cabinet and, through it, to Parliament, a deliberate production and investment policy, for a group of large combines or a welter of small firms. In so far as freedom depends on the ability of a society to determine, within the limits set by nature, the character of the economic régime under which it shall live, it seems reasonable to say that it would be substantially increased.

Economic liberties are neither the only, nor the most important, liberties. The conventional retort to such arguments is to accuse those who advance them of a soul-less materialism. The serfs, it is said, might be less uncomfortable; but, as cogs in the mechanism of an authoritarian state, they would have bartered their dignity as citizens and men—their initiative, their responsibility, their right to live their own lives and wreck them if they pleased—for a shot of morphia in the soul. It is obvious that, if a despotic government enlarges its control over economic affairs, it will use the only methods which it understands, and manage them as a despot.

But why assume despotism? The idea that there is an entity called 'the State' which possesses, in virtue of its title, uniform characteristics, existing independently of the varying histories, economic environments, constitutional arrangements, legal systems and social psychologies of particular states, and that these characteristics necessarily combine the manners of a Japanese customs official with the morals of a human tiger, is a pure superstition. It is a piece of mysticism pardonable in persons brought up on their knees before some mortal god, but which—if the irreverence may be permitted—is, none the less, a bluff. Half a century ago, when we were informed by philosophers fed on Hegel that the State represented our high selves, it was an optimistic bluff. Today, when we are periodically told that the State is the executive of the capitalist class or—more terrifying still—the product of one of the nastier Freudian complexes, it is a pessimistic bluff. But it is a bluff in either case.

The State is an important instrument; hence the struggle to control it. But it is an instrument, and nothing more. Fools will use it, when they can, for foolish ends, and criminals for criminal ends. Sensible and decent men will use it for ends which are sensible and decent. We, in England, have repeatedly re-made the State, and are re-making it now, and shall re-make it again. Why, in heaven's name, should we be afraid of it? The faithful animal—to vary the metaphor—will run our errands; fetch and carry for us; convey us on our journeys; attend our sick-beds; mind our children; show, on the rare occasions that we tell him, a handsome mouthful of sharp teeth, and generally behave like a useful and well-conducted cur. If he does not do his tricks nicely, we are quite capable of beating our own dog ourselves, as—to do him justice—he is well aware. It is really too much to expect us, at this time o. day, to relapse into hysterics because some nervous professor has decided, on grounds of high theory, that the harmless and obedient creatures, whom we have cursed, kicked and fondled all our lives, is in reality, not a dog at all, but a ferocious species of Siberian wolf.

The truth is that these paroxysms of alarm at the menace to individual freedom involved in every fresh extension of the activities of public bodies are the product of an authoritarian nightmare which, in countries so unfortunate as not yet to have taught their rulers that they are servants, not masters, has only too much justification, but which a mature democracy should have outgrown. Civil liberty depends on freedom of worship; freedom of speech and writing; freedom of meeting; freedom in the choice of occupations; and freedom to combine. Political liberty depends partly on civil liberty, partly on the existence of constitutional arrangements for the maintenance of representative and responsible Government. The sole security for the preservation of either is a public opinion which is determined to preserve them. There is no reason whatever for regarding that security as likely to be weakened merely because steps are taken, as they have been in Great Britain, to extend to the whole population opportunities of well-being previously restricted to a minority; or because certain industries, formerly conducted for the profit of shareholders, are owned and administered by public authorities; or as the result of a decision by a Cabinet responsible to a popularly elected chamber that the national interest will best be served by treating some requirements, rather than others, as possessing the first claim on national resources.

The nostalgic self-deception which, here and there, looks back on the days before the deluge, with their exclusive felicities and securely-guarded comforts, as a golden age of freedom, is not a matter for surprise. It is improbable that the majority of British wage-earners, who recall an unemployment rate averaging, from 1921 to 1938, approximately one-seventh of all insured workers, view the blessings of that happy period in quite the same light. Not by impairing traditional liberties, but by resolution in using them, they have taken in the last three years the first steps towards the attainment of objectives long proclaimed and long resisted. They regard, it may be suspected, full employment, expanded social services, and the transference of foundation industries to public ownership, less as a curtailment of freedom than as an enlargement of it.

IV

In public affairs, as in humbler departments of human life, questions of ends and questions of means inevitably intersect. Disputes as to the former commonly produce more sparks than light, and more heat than either. If a man affirms that his heart leaps up at the spectacle either of a society in which the common good is defined by the decisions of a totalitarian bureaucracy, or of one, like—to mention only one example—the England of a century ago, where, in the unceasing struggle of individuals for personal gain, a conception of the common good cannot easily find a foothold, it may readily be admitted that no logic exists which can prove these exhilarating palpitations to be either right or wrong. One cannot argue with the choice of a soul; and, if he likes that kind of dog, then that is the kind of dog he likes. Most socialists would agree that there may well be nations whose history, conditions and mentality are such that one or other of these types of policy is, for the time being, that best suited to them, and, if so, will wish them such success as their way of life allows. They think it more important, however, to set their own house in order than to watch at the window for topics on which they can lecture their neighbours. They have work to do, and more work, in Great Britain, than can easily be done. They are content, while Pharisees and Sadducees belabour each other and them, to devote their energies to doing it.

The nature of politics, which is one, though only one, of the instruments by which that work is carried on, seems to them less recondite than might be inferred from the utterances of some of the philosophers who discourse upon them. Politics are, or ought to be, the art of achieving by collective action

166

those ends which individuals cannot achieve, or cannot achieve with the same measure of success, by their isolated efforts. We in England think that, in the present situation of the country, co-operative action is likely, in several fields, to produce better results than the nose for money and the scramble to secure it which our grandfathers applauded under the name of free enterprise, and which some of our benevolent neighbours, from the goodness of their generous hearts, now commend to us as a novel invention recently patented by themselves. But, though British socialism is by no means indifferent to economic considerations, its foundations are ethical. Even if the way of co-operation did not yield all the economic advantages expected from it, we should continue to choose it. Both the type of individual character and the style of social existence fostered by it are those which we prefer.

A reasonable level of material wealth is, of course, on its own plane, important, provided that men do not insist—as too often they do—on turning it into a devil, by worshipping it as a god. But it is important as a means, not as an end. Civilization is a matter, not of quantity of possessions, but of quality of life. It is to be judged, not by the output of goods and services per head, but by the use which is made of them. A society which values public welfare above private display; which, though relatively poor, makes the first charge on its small resources the establishment for all of the conditions of a vigorous and self-respecting existence; which gives a high place among those conditions to the activities of the spirit and the services which promote them; which holds that the most important aspect of human beings is not the external differences of income and circumstance that divide them, but the common humanity that unites them, and which strives, therefore, to reduce such differences to the position of insignificance that rightly belongs to them—such a society may be far from what it should be, but it has, at least, set its face towards the light. It is such a society which British socialists are labouring to create.

BRITISH SOCIALISM TODAY[1]

As an organized movement, British Socialism has now two-thirds of a century behind it. Let me begin, at the cost of labouring platitudes, by referring to some parts of the legacy which, in my judgment, will and ought to stand. In the first place, as far as the rank and file are concerned, the impulse behind the movement has been obstinately and unashamedly ethical. The revolt of ordinary men against Capitalism has had its source neither in its obvious deficiencies as an economic engine, nor in the conviction that it represents a stage of social evolution now outgrown, but in the straightforward hatred of a system which stunts personality and corrupts human relations by permitting the use of man by man as an instrument of pecuniary gain. The socialist society envisaged by them is not a herd of tame, well-nourished animals, with wise keepers in command. It is a community of responsible men and women working without fear in comradeship for common ends, all of whom can grow to their full stature, develop to the utmost limit the varying capacities with which nature has endowed them, and—since virtue should not be too austere—have their fling when they feel like it.

British Socialism, in the second place, has regarded institutions as existing for men, not men for institutions. It has not deified the state, but, while extending its sphere of action, has continued to see it, not as a master, but as a serviceable drudge. It has held that the ultimate tribunal by which all forms of organization and policy are to be tried is the conscience of individuals. In presenting its case, it has appealed not merely to economic interests (though such

---

[1] First appeared as an article in *Socialist Commentary*, June 1952.

appeals have their place) but to sentiments of human dignity, justice and equality transcending them.

Thirdly, the British movement has valued democracy, with its corollaries of freedom of speech, writing, worship and meeting, not merely as the sole political method discovered by man of effecting bloodless change, but as a style of life, thought and conduct admirable in itself. It has visualized Socialism, therefore, not as the antithesis of democracy, but as the extension of democratic principles and methods into spheres of life which in the past escaped them.

Finally, the structure of the movement has been of a piece with its premises. Unlike some of the continental versions of Socialism, it was not poured into doctrinal moulds prepared, when the Industrial Revolution was still young, by political theorists and men of letters. It developed as the product of a fusion between the experience of an already vigorous trade unionism and the work of organizations and individuals, like the Fabian Society and the Webbs, engaged in the empirical *terre-à-terre* investigation of capitalist diseases and the remedies for them. The trade union basis has been criticized, but its advantages, in my judgment, outweigh its drawbacks. It has ensured that Socialism in this country rests on broad popular foundations; has averted the deadly disease of dogmatic petrification which afflicted the pre-1914 German Social Democrats; and has saved British Socialism from the sterility which condemns to impotence a party, like the French, severed from working-class roots.

All this, I am of course well aware, will be dismissed as a deplorable revelation of bourgeois Philistinism; but I remain unrepentant. I think that political, as well as other, truths concealed from the wise and learned are apt to be revealed to babes. As far as the principles, though not the techniques for applying them, are concerned, I put my money on the latter. Bludgeoned by my enlightened friends with philosophies of history, which unless a man unfeignedly believe, he cannot as a socialist be saved, I listen with admiring but unconverted awe. My attitude to them remains that expressed in the reply of the wise little girl in a London school asked by her teacher to explain the use of pins: 'Pins are very useful little things; they have saved many people's lives by not a-swollerin' of them.'

The foundation of Socialism is, in my view, a decision that certain types of life and society are fit for human beings and others not. I do not believe that any alchemy exists by which historical facts and tendencies can either be made a substitute for such judgments of value or directly converted into them. I do not share Marx's mid-Victorian conviction of the inevitability of progress; nor do I regard social development as an automatically ascending spiral with Socialism as its climax. On the contrary, I think that, in the absence of sustained and strenuous efforts, the way is as likely to lead down hill as up, and that Socialism, if achieved, will be the creation, not of any mystical historical necessities, but of the energy of human minds and wills. The chicanery, discreetly termed relativism, which dismisses ordinary human virtues, from honesty to mercy, as bourgeois morality; falsifies ethical standards; and applauds as triumphs of proletarian heroism on one side of a frontier episodes denounced by it as Fascist atrocities on the other, appears to me nauseous. I regard it, not as the example of up-to-date realism boasted by its votaries, but as a long-familiar poison.

It must be recognized, finally, that there are nations with histories so tragic and environmental difficulties so immense that some form of authoritarian régime may well be the best of which for the time being they are capable. We have committed too many crimes ourselves to be critical of our neighbours; and, provided that such states are willing to live and let live, British Socialists should wish them such success as political systems of the kind allow. But the pretence that the resulting police collectivisms are a shining example for Western Socialists to follow, when not mere cynical bluff, is either ignorance or a credulity so extreme as to require, not argument, but a doctor. The view that Socialism consists in socializing everything except political authority, on which all else depends, is puerile. The question for Socialists is not merely whether the state owns and controls the means of production. It is also, and even more important, who owns and controls the state. Democracy, in one form or another, is, in short, not merely one of several alternative methods of establishing a Socialist commonwealth. It is an essential condition of such a commonwealth's existence.

I hold, therefore, that in its adherence to these obvious truths, British Socialism has advanced on lines which not only are those alone possible in this country, but are superior in themselves to any alternative yet in view. The strategy and tactics of its struggle with Capitalism are, of course, a different problem. Webb's *Labour and the New Social Order* of 1919 fixed for the next two decades their general design. Particular parts of the programme were later hammered out by him and other members of the Party, with occasional judicious thefts from other sources. In so far as they were concerned with means, not ends, they were necessarily liable to change, as circumstances altered and experience increased.

The post-war Labour Government acted on the resulting policies with remarkable fidelity, and, in my view, with impressive success. Full employment, not, indeed, established by it, but maintained by it in circumstances in which its Conservative opponents would have been tempted to end it, changed the whole quality of life for countless industrial workers, whether they themselves had been unemployed or not. The transfer of half a dozen key services to public ownership may not have greatly affected the distribution of incomes, though in time it will, but it altered the balance of economic power. The combined effects of taxation and of the expansion of communal provision by way of social services were equally marked. With prices moving as they are, statements as to incomes and their distribution are out of date before made. The fact remains that, on the evidence of Mr Rowntree's book,[1] published in 1951, the percentage of persons in York living in poverty had fallen from approximately thirty-one per cent in 1936 to under three per cent in 1950, and that, but for the social legislation of the intervening period, the latter figure would have been, not under one-thirtieth, but over one-fifth.

On the degree to which inequality was diminished it is more difficult to speak. All that can be said is that the extension of social provision has somewhat reduced inequalities of circumstance, in respect, for example, of health, education and security, and that, while disparities of pecuniary income remain shocking, they also appear to have somewhat decreased. The spread between the average income in the highest and the

[1] *Poverty and the Welfare State*, B. Seebohm Rowntree and G. R. Lavers (Longmans).

lowest income-group was in 1938 such that the former was approximately twenty-eight times the latter. In 1948, the gap, though still astonishing, had narrowed to about thirteen times. In 1938, the share of the national income taken, after direct taxation, by the recipients of rent, interest, profits and professional earnings was thirty-four per cent; by 1948 it had fallen to twenty-eight per cent. At the first date, the share going to wages, also after taxation, was thirty-nine per cent; by the second it had risen to forty-eight.

Finally, apart from these specific improvements, the experience of 1945–50 established, I think one important point. It showed that a capitalist economy is not the solid, monolithic block, to be endured as a whole, or overthrown as a whole, that some simpletons suggested. It proved that a Socialist Government, with the public behind it, can change the power relations within the system, can ensure that a larger part of the resources yielded by it are devoted to raising the standard of life of the mass of the population, and can compel those directing it to work on lines which, left to themselves, they would not choose.

It is true, of course, that what a Socialist Government has done a Conservative successor can and will in part undo. The only infallible recipe for preventing political heirs from dissipating the estate is to ensure that there shall be none. But that remedy, which can as easily be used against Socialists as by them, is worse than the disease. A Socialist Government will, in due course, be again returned to power. The important thing is that the programme on which then it acts should have been thoroughly discussed and sifted before the moment for its application comes.

I have no qualifications for formulating such a programme. Some of the measures contained in it will, no doubt, fall within the four corners of what may be called conventional Socialist policy. I assume that the holes torn by our opponents in the social services will be repaired; that the task of maintaining full employment, which was one of the capital achievements of the last Labour Government, will receive not less attention from the next; and that the removal of successive segments of industrial life from direction by profit-making entrepreneurs or their servants will be carried forward, though not necessarily by the methods or with the organization hitherto adopted. The redistributive measures of 1945–50 were effective as regards income, and it may be doubted whether much more on these lines can in present circumstances be done; but, apart from the increase in death duties—from, for example, fifty to eighty per cent on estates of £1,000,000 and over—the ownership of capital, with all the power and privileges conferred by it, remains almost intact.

The exemption from taxation of gains arising from capital appreciation seems to me about as rational as a close season for sharks. A tax abstracting a substantial part of them is overdue, but it would leave the problem of past accumulations untouched. The two most massive pillars of indefensible inequalities are inheritance and education. It is an extraordinary fact that, after half a century or more of death duties, fifty per cent of the country's wealth is still owned by one per cent of the population. On this point the next Labour Government should, in my opinion, go all out. A low maximum should be fixed (e.g. £25,000 to £50,000) for wealth to be transmitted to heirs, and everything above it should be taxed 100 per cent. The problems of preventing the expenditure of capital as income during the lifetime of the owner, the distribution of property *inter vivos*, and so on, are genuine enough; but I do not believe that, if ordered to do the job, the experts of Somerset House will find such difficulties insurmountable. If they are, the alternative which remains is a capital levy imposed at short notice, and accompanied, to soften the shock, by arrangements for paying during the lifetime of existing owners part of their incomes to them. Whether such a measure is politically practicable depends on the imponderables of public opinion. It is possible that the alarm aroused, not only among a handful of plutocrats, but among the working population, large members of whom, if proletarians at all, are in small way propertied ones, might make the game not worth the candle.

Such measures, with the possible exception of the last, are in principle common form. The question, I suppose, is the additions to be made to them. In considering it, the first need, it seems to me, is to treat sanctified formulae with judicious irreverence and to start by deciding what precisely is the end in view. As far as the mere externals of economic structure and organization are concerned, our aim, I imagine, is to ensure that limited resources are used in the general interest to meet social needs in the order of their relative importance, and that the crucial decisions determining the degree to which that object is attained shall be taken, not by persons responsible to no one but themselves or—in theory—to their shareholders, but by public authorities who can be called to account. It should be recognized that the attainment of that objective is not merely compatible with the use of a variety of different means, but actually requires it. The statement often made by our opponents that the sole distinctive feature of Socialist policy is nationalization is ludicrously beside the mark. In reality, the Socialist arsenal contains a diversity of different weapons, among which nationalization has an important place. The essential point, however, is that full and effective use should be made of all.

Applied in suitable circumstances, nationalization possesses genuine virtues. The mere transference of property-rights involved in it is not by itself tidings of great joy. It is important less for what it does than for what it makes it possible to do. It provides a clear space, free from the obstructive jungle of private interests, on which to build. It facilitates, therefore, the substitution of intelligent staffwork at the top and co-operative labour throughout, for a competitive scramble or monopolistic restrictionism. The unification on a national basis hitherto adopted may, in some or many cases, be the right design. Against its advantages, however, must be set certain drawbacks. The danger of top-heavy bureaucracy and remote control is, in my opinion, genuine. Effective supervision of these Leviathans by public and parliament has hardly yet been established. Though directors in nationalized industries do not swindle workers, the gulf between the brass-hats and the industrial PBI still too often remains profound.

Finally, Socialism ought to mean something vital and inspiring in the lives of the great majority of workers. The social and full employment policies of the Labour Government did, I think, come home to them. I doubt whether its industrial policy, which to most of them was a spectacle, rather than a personal experience, did. Since the number of industries ready for prompt nationalization is limited, I question whether, unless enlarged, it can.

I am in favour, therefore, of extending, with the necessary improvements, public ownership and management by national boards and corporations, as and when practicable. But I think that that particular arrangement should be regarded, not as the one essential element in Socialist policy, pending the application of which nothing valuable can be done, but merely as one species of a large genus of expedients for bringing economic enterprise under social control, and that, instead of ignoring other members of the family, we should labour to stimulate their growth. There are some undertakings which it may not at present be possible to nationalize outright, but which nevertheless it is important to harness to public ends. It is a question whether, in the case of public companies, the government should not be given the right to appoint a proportion of the directors. In many, perhaps in most, cases, it might not deem it necessary to exercise that right, but on some it would, and the knowledge that such a power of inside control existed would be a salutary influence on all.

Since the war public money has been used to build in the Development Areas factories to be leased to private firms. There does not seem to be any reason why similar facilities should not deliberately be extended to groups of undertakings organized on Socialist and co-operative lines. Local authorities are buyers on a great scale of furniture, building requisites, stationery, catering equipment and so on. As the Socialist hold on local government strengthens, the obvious course for such authorities would seem to be the establishment by joint action between them of productive works for self-supply. The infinite diversities of the building industry—a few large firms of national importance with a multitude of minor local units—may preclude conventional patterns of public ownership; but to combine the nationalization of the former with some form of co-operative organization of the latter ought not to be beyond the wit of man. It is needless, however, to multiply examples, of which many better ones, doubtless, could be found. The point is that, without neglecting new departures in nationalization, we ought to think, not in terms of a single bottle-neck through which Socialist re-organization must be forced, but of a multitude of growing points, at each of which a Socialist government can bring its influence to bear.

Matters of this kind—industrial organization and control—are, after all, no more than machinery. What matters most is the kind of life which people lead and the satisfaction which they find in it. And here, I suspect, most of us are apt to think too much of problems and too little of persons; too much in terms of evils to be cured, and too little of happiness to be increased; too much of facts which can be counted, measured and weighed, too little of the human imponderables, which cannot. Our scandalous failure to remedy the urban housing shortage, with the consequent inability of tenants to resist exploitation by landlords, is one example, and the world of industry offers several more. What men want, it seems to me, is not merely a fair deal in pecuniary matters—though, of course they want that—but security, decent conditions, comradeship in work, the right, subject to getting their job done, to do it in their own way, without being badgered and bossed about; the consideration for their convenience and respect for their opinions which makes a man feel that he counts; and an equal chance, irrespective of income, for themselves and, still more, for their children, to make the most of what is in them. As far as the daily routine of life is concerned, it is in these pedestrian requisites that the substance of such venerable abstractions as Liberty and Equality consists. The Labour Government contributed something, though not enough, to both; but it was stronger, it seems to me, in dealing with the constitutional superstructure than with the economic and psychological foundations. It increased freedom by enlarging the range of alternatives between which ordinary men can choose; but it did little to remove from wage-earners the sense that they belong to a class treated as instruments for ends dictated from above. It did not attempt, in short, to grapple with the problem of changing their economic status. If Socialism is to be an inspiring force in daily life, that problem is vital.

I do not pretend to possess a formula for solving it. Conditions vary so widely from one industry to another, that I doubt whether any general solution of universal application exists; but the direction in which one would desire to move can hardly be in doubt. The brutal truth is that down to 1939 the economic system was kept running by hunger and fear. A decade of full employment largely destroyed the conditions on which that barbarous discipline depended. The proper alternative to it, whether full employment exists or not, is the assumption of increased responsibilities for productive efficiency by the workers themselves. The difficulty here—to speak frankly—is not merely the recalcitrance of employers. It is the apathy and torpor of many workers, who in theory desire freedom, but who in practice are too often reluctant to assume the burdens without which freedom cannot be had.

If a Socialist government means business—if it intends to create an economic system socialist all through, and not merely at the top—then it must take the initiative, force the pace, and—I won't say compel—but persuade men to be free. It should use the industries in public ownership as a laboratory where different methods of making industrial democracy a reality are tested, and should insist that those who direct them should devote as much attention to promoting experiments with that end in view as they do to technical improvements. Exorbitant salaries may have been inevitable at the start; but they corrupt *morale* and ought to go. There is already, I think, representation of workers on the authorities concerned, at the regional and national levels, but that is not sufficient. In individual establishments there should be a systematic attempt to democratize the practical routine of industrial life by transferring to bodies representing the wage-earners such functions as the allocation of jobs within a working group; the appointment of leaders in charge of them; and matters relating to promotion, dismissal and disciplinary measures. Trade union approval and co-operation would, of course, be a necessity; but the changes required are, in principle, little more than an enlargement in the scope of collective bargaining. In these matters, the industries already nationalized should clearly be the pioneers, and particular plants controlled by them might well be allotted the function of serving as experimental stations. If a Socialist government really intends to establish a new status for wage-earners, it should obviously begin with these industries, since it is for these that it is already directly responsible.

The question of status has another aspect. A formula sometimes hailed by Socialists as the watch-word of a new order is
Equality of Opportunity; but the phrase may express either of
two distinct—and sometimes, though not always, antithetic—
ideals. The opportunities which it is desired to equalize may
be opportunities to rise; to get on; to exchange one position
for a succession of others; to climb, in the conventional metaphor, the educational or economic ladder. Or they may be
opportunities to lead a good life, in all senses of the term,
whether one 'rises' or not. The emphasis of the former interpretation of the phrase is on mobility. Its aim is the establishment
of conditions which offer the maximum scope for individual
self-advancement. The emphasis of the latter is on solidarity.
The society sought by it is one in which, while individuals are
free to follow the bent of their talents or tastes, the impulse to
seek a new position is not sharpened by exasperation at
unnecessary disabilities attaching to that already held, and in
which the majority of men are happy to continue in familiar
surroundings, because they enjoy in them, not only the economic security, but the dignity, the social contacts, and, if they
please, the intellectual interests and culture, which human
nature demands. The sentiment of the father who hopes—too
often, as things are, with reason—that his son will follow any
trade but his own illustrates the first view. The attitude of the
worker who refuses a foreman's job because it would divide
him from his mates illustrates the second.

Individuals deprived of the chance to use their powers as
they please suffer from frustration. Further, society cannot
afford more than a certain proportion of fools in high places,
which in England is already—to speak with moderation—
sufficiently large, and must draw, if its directive work is to
be efficiently done, on a broad stream of talent from below.
For both reasons arrangements facilitating vertical mobility
are important. It is equally or more essential, however, that
the mass of mankind, who, for obvious statistical reasons,
cannot perform athletic feats in scaling social heights, should
enjoy a high standard of civilization. Nothing could be more
remote from Socialist ideals than the competitive scramble of
a society which pays lip-service to equality, but too often means
by it merely equal opportunities of becoming unequal. Our

aim should be the opposite. It should be to effect a complete divorce between differences of pecuniary income and differences in respect of health, security, amenity of environment, culture, social status and esteem. Might it not, indeed, be beneficial, not only to destroy the connection between them existing today, but to reverse it, so as to make it contemptible to be rich and honourable to be poor? On that state of super-blessedness, however, I must not now dwell.

Such an attitude would mean that our main emphasis should be laid, not on enlarging the meshes of selective sieves, but on raising the standards of universal provision. Its practical application can best be illustrated, perhaps, from the sphere of education. During the last generation educational progress has been too often envisaged predominantly in terms of a more generous selection of exceptional capacity for intensive cultivation. The Labour Government inherited that tradition, and applied it on a scale unknown in the past. The results have been beneficial, but a change of emphasis is overdue.

Public education originated in England as the discipline of a supposedly inferior class, which happened to comprise the great majority of the nation. In practice, though not in theory, that disastrous legacy still clings to it. Much primary school accommodation is a disgrace, demanding widespread clearance and reconstruction. A revolution in staffing which will reduce to a maximum of thirty the number of children allowed in a class is long over-due. The secondary education of the majority of children is now given in the Secondary Modern School. Some brilliant examples of such schools exist; but many of them still remain, it is to be feared, the old elementary schools called by another name. Because of the traditional superiority of the particular kind of secondary school known as a grammar school, the struggle to win a place in it is intense, with the result of disillusionment for those who fail and over-pressure on all. No amount of scholarship provision can take the place of a drastic improvement in the quality of primary education accompanied by the prolongation of the secondary school life of all to sixteen. The latter policy has been strongly urged in the Crowther Report.[1] Unless its application is to be postponed to

[1] *15 to 18*. Report of the Central Advisory Council on Education, 1959. Tawney added this reference in the revised edition of this essay.

a distant future, preparations for carrying it out must, as the Report was at pains to emphasize, be made at once.

Special difficulties of money, material and personnel are, as usual, said to impede improvements; but the evils to be cured were rampant and well known long before such difficulties arose, and at a period when, given the will, they could easily have been removed. The fundamental cause of their existence is the corrupting influence of a false standard of values, which perverts, not only education, but wide tracts of thought and life. It is this demon—the idolatry of money and success— with whom, not in one sphere alone but in all, including our own hearts and minds, Socialists have to grapple.

PART IV
LITERATURE

12

SOCIAL HISTORY AND LITERATURE[1]

In a famous passage of the *Inferno* Ulysses speaks to Dante and Vergil of 'the passion to win experience of the world and of human vice and worth', which drove him when, after his twenty years of wandering he had at length reached home, once more to set sail on his last fatal voyage. Whatever else the world may contain, man's relations with nature, his commerce with his fellows, and the convictions, aspirations and emotions composing his inner life, are for us, as for the poet, its capital constituents. No one can be fully at home either with it or with himself until, through the vicarious experience of which the vehicle is books, he has learned enough of the triumphs and tragedies of mankind to catch a glimpse of the heights to which human nature can rise and depths to which it can sink. To such comprehension, which less enlightened ages call wisdom, there is more than one road; but an acquaintance which, for most of us, only reading can convey with the methods by which men of like passions with ourselves have wrestled, in circumstances different from our own, with problems of individual and collective existence—religion, law and government, the conquest of the material environment and the ordering of social life—that are also ours, can make a modest contribution to it. It is part of the process by which we surmount the limitations of our isolated personalities and become partners in a universe of interests which we share with humanity.

Not the least potent of the magicians who fling wide the windows opening on these vistas are the Muses who preside over History and Literature. Each rules a separate province, with laws of its own; but the debatable land where they intercommon is not small; and, like terrestrial states, their immaterial

[1] Lecture delivered to the National Book League, 25.10.49. Printed as a pamphlet by the Cambridge University Press and reproduced by courtesy of the NBL.

kingdoms flourish best when friendly intercourse between them is unimpeded by artificial barriers. Naturally, neither is without its riddles; and both offer ample opportunities for finished exhibitions of the great art of complicating the simple and obscuring the obvious by which the authentic intellectual proves his title to that proud name. I observe these gymnastics with admiration and awe; but a consciousness that the stratosphere is not my spiritual home deters me from imitating them. So, without attempting to add yet another to the philosophical rationalizations of activities which, if not as old as man, are in one form or another, coeval with his earliest written records, let me turn to my theme.

The humble branch of history, with which alone this evening I am concerned, cannot boast, like some of its more illustrious colleagues, that it supplies precedents and warnings of immediate utility in the conduct of great affairs. But the forces that figure most conspicuously before the footlights are not always those that set the stage; and, if studies dealing in the prose of common life neither breakfast with ministers nor dine at international conferences, they are not necessarily, for that reason, to be consigned to the limbo reserved for triviality. Each generation must write its history for itself, and draw its own deductions from that already written, not because the conclusions of its predecessors are untrue, but for a practical reason. Different answers are required, because different questions are asked. Standing at a new point on the road, it finds that fresh ranges of the landscape come into view, whose unfamiliar intricacies demand an amplification of traditional charts.

It is obviously not an accident that when, after 1830, French thinkers reflected on the convulsions of the four preceding decades, the result should have been the search for the hidden cracks and fissures in the social order demolished by the earthquake, of which de Tocqueville's *L'Ancien Régime* remains a lofty landmark; or that England in the full tide of the Industrial Revolution should have provided Macaulay with the foil against which to throw into high relief, in his famous third chapter, the simpler society of an age politically brilliant, but, compared with his own, economically immature; or that the year of revolutions, in which his book appeared, should also have seen a less sanguine interpretation of the material triumphs applauded by him begin, in the obscurity of a cheap pamphlet, a voyage that was to take it round the world; or that when, after 1870, the great industry and an urban civilization were in process of conversion from an insular peculiarity into European institutions, scholars of different nationalities and opposing views should have launched, with resources of knowledge and criticism not available to Marx, a debate on the historical origins of Capitalism which is not yet concluded. It was equally natural that a generation increasingly conscious of the problems posed by the profound changes in human relations which those movements had produced, should turn, with heightened curiosity, to works revealing the life of societies not yet affected by them or experiencing only their first disturbing impact.

Of the contributions of authors with widely varying interests —legal historians, writers whose interests were primarily economic, students of the development of local government and administration, experts on the history of particular localities, later geographers and ecologists—I must not pause to speak. By the end of the last century, not a few obscure departments of social life had been compelled to yield their secrets, and the doors into others since then unlocked have not been few. The adjective in my title is to be regarded, therefore, not as a signpost pointing to a recently discovered field, but merely as a reminder of riches already at our disposal, or waiting to be extracted from ground beneath our feet. All history has as its theme one aspect or another of collective life; and the function of Social History—if that term is to be employed—is not the enrolment of an additional recruit in the battalion of specialisms already at work. It is primarily, I suppose, to underline the truth that, if research requires a division of forces, a humane education requires a synthesis, however provisional, of the results of their labours, and to encourage us, by seeing those results, not as isolated fragments, but as connected parts of a body of living tissue, to acquire a more synoptic and realistic view of the activities composing the life of society. The subject, as I interpret it, is concerned not merely or mainly with the iridescent surface of manners, fashions, social conventions and intercourse, but with the unseen foundations, which, till they shift or crumble, most men in most generations are wont to take for granted. Nor, since human beings cannot live on air and rarely live alone, can public and private business—politics and economics—be excluded from its scope. These restless energumens are never so potent as when ignored; and notices to quit served on them in a preface rarely deter the pertinacious trespassers from slinking back into the text. The sensible course is to welcome them from the start as partners in a story which, the world being what it is, they have necessarily done much to shape.

Social history, thus conceived, can be approached by several paths. One, not the least pleasant and instructive, which starts from some familiar scene of daily life, I must not do more than mention. There are countries so unfortunate that a traveller can journey in them for several days with no companion but nature, who is delightful, but not, by herself, sufficient. England, like most of her European neighbours, is not among them. As in Mr Chesterton's poem, it is 'an island like a little book, full of a thousand tales'. Something amusing or tragic has occurred at every corner; sweat, in the famous phrase, not to mention blood and tears, is thick on most of it. There are worse points of departure for history and those who teach it than the visible realities to which such associations cling.

Some of them, I suppose, are treasured memories to most of us; and, of a hundred illustrations, one miniature must suffice. A tump—what the cultured call a *tumulus*—with neolithic bones which the aged roadman at last consented not to throw away; a precipitate lane beside it, known to the natives, though not to writers of guide-books, as King Charles' Hill, because, on an early day in August, 1643, some enterprising staff officer contrived—Heaven knows how—to get the army down it on its way to the siege of the godly city the unforeseen tenacity of whose obstinate shopkeepers wrecked the year's campaign; twenty minutes one way the room in which, forty years before, the Catholic Throckmorton of the day had brooded with Catesby over projects for the famous plot; twenty minutes the other the farm called Abbey Farm, seized, two generations earlier, by the Defender of the Faith from a local religious house; a mile north the high point known as Wittentree

Clump, where the wise men of the district are thought to have assembled in Saxon times and the Home Guard met in our own; a mile east a village not finally enclosed till the sixties of last century, in circumstances some of which—characteristically, the comic, not the sad—twenty years ago old men still recounted; a mile south the magnificent wrought-iron gates of the Haunted House, the work—so the probably mendacious story runs—of a smith convicted for murder, whom a wicked judge consented to spare, on condition that he made them, and then, when they were made, proceeded to hang; in the distance the hill from which, Mr Madden[1] has told us, Clement Perks of the Hill, in *Henry IV*, took his designation, with the hamlet at its foot inhabited by the 'arrant knave' favoured by Mr Justice Shallow, the name of which is pronounced in the improbable manner in which Shakespeare, who, to judge by his spelling, must have heard it spoken, decided to write it—all, except the last, demand no more than tolerable boots and a longish afternoon.

These human associations are as vital and moving a part of the landscape as its hills and streams. There are many districts, urban not less than rural, as rich or richer in them. If education does not use them, of what use are they? I have never taught children; so, like everyone else in that position, I know exactly how to do it. A one-inch ordnance map as the teacher's bible; an attempt to lead the older of the little victims to see and feel scenes every day beneath their eyes; a few good books, when such exist, in which to read of what they saw; and only then a gradual advance towards wider horizons—such would be some of the ingredients in my prescription.

All this, however, is a digression for which I apologize. Let me return to the more powerful ally invoked in my title, on whom all of us, wherever our lot is cast, can always lean. It seems to be of the nature of scholastic institutions, not least universities, to proliferate to excess in the artificial entities known in the language of the trade as 'subjects'. When we reach years of discretion—which I take to mean the age when

---

[1] D. H. Madden, *The Diary of Master William Silence* (Longmans, Green, 1907, pp. 8, 3–7, 380–3). Madden's identification of 'the hill' with Stinchcombe appears to be accepted by Professor Herford. See *The Works of Shakespeare* (Editor, C. H. Herford, Eversley Edition: Macmillan, 1899–1900, 10 vols. Vol. VI, p. 494 *note*). Woncot (Woodmancote) is now part of Dursley.

youth shows signs of getting over its education—part of our business is to join those naturally connected interests which the demands of examinations and the exigencies of time-tables have temporarily put asunder. The enjoyment of great literature is an end, not a means; and only a barbarian would degrade its timeless truths to the status of materials for a humbler art. But, to the charge of Philistinism, two pleas may be advanced.

Some familiarity, in the first place, with the scenes amid which the masters lived and worked—the disorderly, brilliant, vulgar, little London of the great age of the drama, vivid with the mingled gaiety and squalor of a street in Peiping; the ways of the polite society which idolized Pope; the East Anglian villages beneath whose tranquil surface Crabbe encountered his experiences 'sad as reality and wild as dreams'; the fusion of the traditions of a border region still not wholly tamed with the influence of a city then not the least among the cultural capitals of Europe, which formed the mind of Scott—such knowledge not only is a tribute owed to genius by posterity, but can become, if kept in due subordination in the background of our minds, the foot of a ladder leading into the world of imagination which genius has created. It is equally true, in the second place, and more important for the historian, that literature opens windows on realities that would otherwise elude him. History, it is sometimes said, is concerned with facts; and, facts, Burns has remarked, in a line which I do not venture to quote, but which a friend has translated for me into gratuitously prosaic prose, do not shift their position, but remain unalterably what they are. There are, doubtless, many facts—though not, perhaps, so many as is sometimes supposed—which behave with the propriety ascribed to them by the poet. Some are more elusive monsters, of whom it may be said that to stay put, without entering into unanticipated and embarrassing combinations, is the last thing they can be trusted to do. Not a few are chameleons, which change their colour with the context in which they are seen and the eyes that see them.

To one poet who experienced it, the English Civil War was the vindication of providential justice; to a second, a reluctant soldier, a judgment on a people 'by our lusts disordered into wars'; to a third, a 'cause too good to have been fought for'.[1] The mild and partial counter-revolution called the Restoration meant one thing to the writer of *Pilgrim's Progress*; another to the author of *Absalom and Achitophel*; a third to the Bishop—fat Tom Spratt—who composed the first history of the Royal Society; a fourth to the ex-cabin boy who, after rising to be Professor of Anatomy at Oxford and head of Cromwell's Army Medical Corps in Ireland, helped to found that famous body; showed his mettle by accepting a challenge to a duel, on condition that, since he was short-sighted, it should be fought in a dark cellar, with hatchets as the weapon;[2] and ended as not the least among the pioneers of English economic thought. A reader, if such a person exists, of the philosophical poem by Erasmus Darwin—the grandfather of the famous Charles—on the technological triumphs of his day, who turns from it to the work in which, just over a decade later, Southey described their seamy side, may be pardoned for failing to realize that the same people and period are depicted in both.[3] The first of the five years immediately preceding the second Reform Act saw the work by Ruskin on the social ethics of his fellow-countrymen, the publication of which in the *Cornhill Magazine* was discontinued by Thackeray, then its editor, on the ground that the moral sentiments of his sensitive readers were outraged by it; the third, the novel in which the immortal Mr Podsnap announced the great truth that 'this island is blessed, Sir, by Providence, to the direct exclusion of such other countries as there may happen to be'; the fifth, the classic in which the

---

[1] John Milton, *The Tenure of Kings and Magistrates*, 1649 (Editor, W. T. Allison, New York, 1911), and *A Defence of the People of England*, 1650, see John Milton, *Prose Works* (various publishers); Henry Vaughan, *The Constellation*, see *The Works of Henry Vaughan* (Editor, A. B. Grosart, Fuller Worthies' Library, 1870–1, 4 vols. Vol. I, p. 157), and *Ad Posteros* (*ibid.*, Vol. II, pp. 172–3), and for Vaughan's military service: F. E. Hutchinson, *Henry Vaughan: a Life and Interpretation* (Oxford University Press, 1947, chap. V). The words of Andrew Marvell occur in one of his less exhilarating works. *The Rehearsal Transposed*, see *The Complete Works in Verse and Prose of Andrew Marvell* (Editor, A. B. Grosart, Fuller Worthies' Library, 1872–5, 4 vols. Vol. III, p. 212).
[2] Sir William Petty's acceptance of the challenge is recounted by Evelyn, see *Diary and Correspondence of John Evelyn* (Editor, William Bray, Colburn, 1850–2, 4 vols. Vol. II, p. 96; Vol. III, p. 392).
[3] Erasmus Darwin, *The Botanic Garden: a Poem in two Parts*. Part I, *The Economy of Vegetation;* Part II, *The Loves of the Plants, with philosophical notes* (London, 1794–5, 2 vols.); Robert Southey, *Letters from England* (London, 1807, 3 vols. Vol. I, pp. 303–8; Vol. II, pp. 139–53; Vol. III, pp. 132–4).

constitution of the chosen people was expounded by Bagehot, not without some hints, developed more at length in a later edition, that its best days might be over.[1]

The facts which elicited these diverse responses were obviously, in some sense, the same; but, not less obviously, they break into a hundred different facets. In order to understand the situations composed by clusters of them, it is necessary to undertake a voyage of circumnavigation, which enables the ambiguous mass to be seen and probed from different angles. Clever *litterateurs*, all glitter and fizz, are the worst company in which to make it; great authors are the best. Experiencing the agonies of the *mêlée*, but with the strength to stand above it, they grasp as a whole realities which those in the line see only in fragments, and often—battles being, in this respect, what they always have been and always must be—do not see at all. More important, their vision is sharpened by an emotional receptiveness which lesser mortals lack. All branches of history present enigmas, which only labour can unravel. The sciolism which finds in infallible formulae of universal application a painless alternative to thought need not be considered, but even honest work is not without its snares. The analogy of some other sciences make it natural that some of those engaged in history should be preoccupied, at times to excess, with questions of change, development and causation. That approach has its uses, but to view either an individual or a society primarily as a problem is to make certain of misconceiving them. Sympathy is a form of knowledge. It cannot be taught. It can only be absorbed by association with those the depth of whose natures has enabled them most profoundly to feel and most adequately to express it.

Generalities are unconvincing. Let me endeavour to illustrate these commonplaces by glancing for a moment at the society and literature of a period whose epic quality no later discoveries or re-interpretations are likely to impair. The duration to be assigned to the Elizabethan age varies with the aspect of its existence which is under consideration. It is

[1] John Ruskin, *Unto this Last: Four Essays on the First Principles of Political Economy* (Smith Elder, *now* Murray, 1862), and J. A. Hobson, *John Ruskin, Social Reformer* (Nisbet, 1898, p. 42); Charles Dickens, *Our Mutual Friend*, 1864–5 (various publishers), and William Bagehot, *The English Constitution*, 1867 (various publishers).

not the same in international as in domestic policies. In literature it is longer than in either; and, as in the case of the Victorian era, the resemblance between the opening and concluding phrases of the reign from which it takes its name are less marked than the contrasts. A mood, an attitude of mind, an outlook on life, can hardly be dated. If, however, a watershed is sought at which earlier doubts of the survival of the *régime* melt into the buoyant self-confidence of its middle years, the collapse, at the end of its first decade, of the last of the feudal and Catholic revolts may be regarded as marking it.

It is at some point in the quarter of a century following that defeat of the old England by the new—the period when stability is assured and tempers, later to be spoiled by depression, the Irish fiasco and the war-taxation resulting from it, not yet set on edge—that the Elizabethan high noon may be said to begin. The phrase itself is of recent origin; but the sentiment expressed by it is not a modern idealization. Within a generation of the death of the Queen, the good days that ended with her were already a legend, to which antagonists soon to be at each others' throats continued to appeal at the moment when they were destroying the conditions that had produced it. The constitutional properties of the majestic past were to be invoked by Hyde; its sage, paternal authoritarianism by Wentworth; its anti-Spanish foreign policy, when that policy was out of date, by the House of Commons, and, later, by Cromwell; the success of its business diplomacy by the chief of the export cartels which spoke for the City; its conservative social reconstruction by the few who voiced the feelings of peasants and craftsmen; its indulgence to buccaneering and the non-commercial virtues by country gentlemen fretting for the golden days before, as one of them wrote, 'peace and law had beggared us all'.[1] The loftiest achievements of the literary movement fall outside the reign in which it began; but the 'eighties, with Sidney's *Apologie for Poetrie* and Marlowe's tragedies, are its magnificent youth; while the appearance in the same decade of Camden's *Britannia* and Hakluyt's *Voyages*, and, in the first year of the next, of the first three books of *The Faerie Queene*, reflects the mood of a generation conscious of

[1] John Oglander, *A Royalist's Note-book. The Commonplace Book of Sir John Oglander of Nunwell*. (Transcribed and edited by Francis Bamford, Constable, 1936, p. 14.)

having done some things worth remembering. When posterity speaks of the Elizabethan age, it is commonly, I suppose, that dazzling outburst of artistic genius that the words first recall.

Legends are apt to be fallacious in detail and true in substance. If the England of Elizabeth has a title to its reputation, the secret of its charm is not to be found in regions where a generation more refined might be disposed first to seek it. It is not humanity; for, judged by the standards of any period less debased than our own, its brutality was shocking. It flogged and branded the unhappy people whom poverty compelled to take the roads. In matters such as Catholic propaganda, where the safety of the state was thought to be at stake, it used torture without compunction. It practised, on occasion, a calculated atrocity in its treatment of the Irish. In England itself, the Northern rising had as its sequel, not only the punishment of great offenders, but an attempt to strike terror by mass executions of humble followers.

Its long suit, again, was not enlightenment. It is needless to speak of its popular superstitions, sometimes innocent and graceful, sometimes barbarous; it is sufficient to recall that the view of the universe which appealed to many able and high-minded men as an improvement on them was that associated with the theology of Calvin. A forbearing and pacific spirit was not among its ornaments. Tempers were hasty; knives loose in the sheath. If, at home, private wars had ceased, private vendettas had not; while, abroad, the heroes of the maritime epic were justly denounced by their victims as pirates. Nor, finally, were saintliness and a reverence for it, which have redeemed some harsh ages, qualities much in esteem. A hard materialism, which saw the world in terms of title-deeds, rent-rolls and profits, was not a vice confined to worldlings. It had conspicuous devotees, not only, as would be expected, in business and at Court, but among the children of light on the episcopal bench.

If, therefore, a man has a taste for heavy shadows, he need not run short of paint. Yet, whatever the improprieties of the magician, his spell somehow works. When everything has been said—and much more might be said—of the horrors of the time, there still floats over it all turbid radiance, which, if difficult to seize and express, is not difficult to feel. The life of that quality is not long—two generations and it is almost dead—but, while it lasts, it is intoxicating. Everyone loves a lover, and it is partly what Arnold meant when, quoting Shakespeare's murderous Richard on the eve of the battle—'Stir with the lark tomorrow, gentle Norfolk'—he spoke of the note of the day as an inexhaustible gusto. It is the enthusiastic, high-spirited zest, enchanted with the world and not at odds with itself, which meets one, not only in the high places of poetry, but on the level plain of intimate letters and casual conversations, and which finds its way into literature because it is already in life.

One hears it in one mood in the lament of one of Burleigh's correspondents on the men who fell in action: 'Consider the thousands of brave English people that have been consumed by sea and land within these two years, [who] have not been rogues, cut-purses, horse-stealers, committers of burglary and other sorts of thieves (as some of our captains and men of war, to excuse themselves, do report) but in truth they were young gentlemen, yeomen and yeomen's sons, and artificers of the most brave sort, such as disdained to pilfer and steal, but went as voluntary to serve of a gaiety and joyalty of mind, all which kind of people are the flower and force of a kingdom.'[1] One hears it in another in the innocent self-satisfaction, saved from arrogance by its artlessness, of Harrison's *Description of Britain*, where not only are 'the artificers and husbandmen . . . so merry without malice and plain without inward Italian and French craft and subtlety that it would do a man good to be in company with them', but the cattle are larger and juicier than in less favoured lands; the mastiffs so humane that, when a parent is about to chastise his child, the generous creature snatches the rod from his hand; and the very mongrels—'whappets and prick-eared curs meet for many toys'—seem to wag their tails twice as fast as ordinary dogs.[2] One encounters

---

[1] Historical Manuscripts Commission, *MSS of the Marquis of Salisbury* (Part IV, pp. 4–5).

[2] William Harrison, *An Historicall description of the Islande of Britayne, etc.*, in Raphael Holinshed, *The firste Volume of the Chronicles of England*, 1577, 1587, etc. (See Book II, chap. VI; Book III, chap. I; Book III, chap. VII of 1587 edition.) A more handy work to use is *Elizabethan England, from a 'Description of England' by William Harrison* (W. Scott, 1889), edited by Lothrop Withington, with an introduction by F. J. Furnivall, which contains selections from Harrison: see especially pp. 94–5, 151–2, 184.

it in a third guise in Nash's surprising rhapsody on the unexciting fish which made the fortune of East Anglian sea-ports—'the puissant red herring, the golden Hesperides red herring, the Maeonian red herring, the red herring of Red Herrings Hall, every pregnant peculiar of whose resplendent laud and honour to delineate and adumbrate to the ample life were a work that would drink four score and eighteen Castalian founts of eloquence, consume another Athens of facunditie, and abate the haughtiest poetical fury between this and the Zone and the Tropic of Cancer. . . . But no more will I spend on it than this: Saint Patrick for Ireland, Saint George for England, and the red herring for Yarmouth'.[1] If, as has been said, the best sign of spiritual health is happiness, then I am unable to resist the conclusion that our benighted ancestors were not far from grace. Perhaps, in view of their crimes, they should have been; but, in these matters, the ways of Providence are notoriously past finding out.

To be charmed by this eager vivacity, sometimes innocent and naïf, often truculent, is not to succumb to the insipid and unplausible idyll of May-poles, merry peasants and benevolent squires. It is obvious that social geology is moulded largely by economic forces. It is obvious also that the composition and lie of the strata, and the weight of the pressure of the upper layers on the lower, reflect the thrusts and strains which such forces produce. It should be equally evident, however, that both the action of material interests and the fabric on which they work are not identical in all environments, but different in each, and that a particular combination of them may be either more or less favourable to social health.

If, for a short time, Elizabethan England was in that respect fortunate, some reasons, at least, are not difficult to suggest. It was a loosely knit, decentralized society, whose pattern of existence was a round of individual activities in a framework fixed by custom. Throughout great areas, especially in the north and west from Cumberland to Devon, land resources abundant in relation to population produced both a moving agricultural frontier and a mentality and style of life which were semi-colonial. In these half-settled regions, the 'wild

[1] Thomas Nashe, *Lenten Stuffe*, see *The Complete Works of Thomas Nashe* (Editor, A. B. Grosart, Huth Library, 1881–5, 6 vols. Vol. V, pp. 307–8).

wood' of the ballads, with its deer, its distinctive crafts, and its opportunities for lawless independence, was not only an economic ally, to whom their inhabitants looked for rough grazing, as well as timber and other forest products, but, in case of need, a trusted friend and refuge. The oft-told tale of *Adam Bell, Clym of the Clough, and William of Cloudeslee* spoke to them of adventures that might well be their own. The Forest of Dean—to give only one example—was an Alsatia into which, when popular feeling ran high, the Sheriff dared not venture. A peasant agitation under Charles, which, after starting in Dorsetshire, travelled *via* Wiltshire to the banks of the Severn, found in that untamed woodland the chance for a last stand.[1] The indignant Privy Councillor who remarked that his Majesty's Government seemed in a fair way to capitulate to a band of resurrected Robin Hoods, spoke more truly than he knew.

Such conditions were, of course, the exception; but almost everywhere outside London, in agriculture, and, except for textiles, in most of the older crafts, the independent producers outnumbered the proletarian elements. Except among the nobility, and often among them, local sentiment was more powerful than class connections; personal relations than the play of the economic mechanism; custom than law; the wisdom of the elders and the lore of the region than stereotyped truths or fallacies standardized for mass consumption. The fact that, outside a few exceptional industries, most men worked for themselves, not for a master, did not make the Mouldys, Bull-Calfs, Feebles and the rest virtuous or even diligent; but it made them individuals, not ciphers. Tradition was a power; and tradition—of its nature, a social creation—set discordant claims and conflicting ambitions against a larger background of mutual comprehension.

On this little intimate world had come in the later sixteenth century an upward movement—the new horizons opened by discovery and, in spite of recurrent depressions, expanding trade; the stimulus to thought given by religious and political controversy; the sensation, as the bad days of the 'forties and

---

[1] S. P. D., Chas. I, CXCIV, 60, I–V; CXCV, 5; CCIII, 7, 36 and 57; CCXV, 57; CCXVI, 42 and 77: P. C. R., 1631, April 5 and 8, June 22, July 16, August 31; 1632, April 4 and 20.

'fifties, with their orgy of aristocratic anarchy, receded into the past, that a corner had been turned, and better times begun. The life-long wage-earners, in most regions a minority, suffered seriously from rising prices; and mere *rentiers*, like some of the old-fashioned nobility, experienced a rough passage, until either they went under, as some of them did, or faced the new realities, rationalized their estate-management, and put their households on a business footing. The *bourgeois* elements in society, which formed the majority—peasants with enough land to produce a small surplus for the market; the more prosperous yeoman, small masters and tradesmen; the gentry who farmed their own lands or leased them to farmers; the business classes generally—had the wind behind them. As often, the immediate and remote results were not the same. The more distant consequence of it all was to impose on the traditional social fabric strains too severe for it to stand; but the first effect was different. It was to give a jolt to the established order strong enough to shake it out of its inertia, but not so violent as to shatter it. It was to arouse sleeping energies and stimulate them to intenser effort, without turning them loose, as two centuries later, to snatch and tear as they pleased.

The Elizabethan age has many different aspects. As a chapter of social history, it is best regarded, perhaps, as the child of that happy interlude between two worlds—between the meaningless ferocities of a feudalism turned senile, such as meet us a century earlier in *The Paston Letters*, and the demure austerities of the first, pious, phase of capitalism. Hence, a gaiety and optimism, which were not merely superficial; a buoyancy as of youth, I will not say slightly intoxicated, but at any rate, in high spirits and at the top of its form. Its secret is energy working in an appreciative environment; an excellence—when there is excellence—not exclusive, but widely shared; a sense of individual achievement, which becomes something more than individual because it is sustained and invigorated by a strong community of sentiment.

Forces later to contend are for the moment in equilibrium. London and its nasty ways are a growing power; but they have not yet overshadowed the provinces. National sentiment is strong; but local life goes its own way. Economic enterprise is expanding; but its requirements have not yet been erected into a final criterion of social expediency. Communal institutions—village, borough and guild—have suffered some rude shocks; but they are still active and vigorous. The Court is a magnet, though, compared with what it was to become, a feeble one; but the outburst of county histories and surveys, which began in the 1570s with Lambard's *Perambulation of Kent*, and which produced a score of similar works in the next half-century, reveals the pride of regional patriotism. Some of the newer industries, which were to dominate the future, are organized from the start on a capitalist basis, but they remain the exception. The character of the traditional productive system, with the few journeymen living, as in the works of Deloney and Dekker, as members of their master's family; the wide distribution of property, which conferred on most men a certain dignity and status; the absence of caste barriers, which made trade a common interest; the fact that money counted more than birth, and for a time favoured new men by levelling old barriers; a common legacy of religious beliefs in which the Reformation, in England a political and social revolution rather than a spiritual upheaval, had made little change—all these influences had combined to produce an outlook on life which was surprisingly homogeneous.

There is a converse fact, which is equally significant, but which I must not pause to develop. It is the enlarged opportunities open to forcible personalities, which make the tragedies of the time, not only on the stage, but in real life—consider, side by side with an Anthony and a Coriolanus, an Essex and a Raleigh—the destruction of greatness by the force of its own genius. The penalties on overweening ambition—'by this sin fell the angels'—are crushing; and, on the whole, it is felt to be right that such penalties should be imposed. Society is aristocratic; but most of its leaders stand too close to the public opinion of their districts to be the arrogant, egotistical oligarchy which later they became. In literature, painting and scholarship, the patron plays an important role; but culture is popular, in the sense that it draws on a body of experience which is not the monopoly of a single class, but is, in some degree, a general possession. It voices the outlook on life, not of an elegant *élite*, but of the world of common men.

The last point is often obscured by our habit of departmentalizing history, but it is not without significance. If any one doubts the connection between the quality of intellectual activities and the dull facts of social systems, let him consider both in two periods which one long lifetime sufficed to span. Few ages have so clearly revealed their soul in their art as that which began with the Restoration and reached its zenith a century later. One may be captivated by that art, or repelled by it, or feel, in different moods, each sentiment in turn; but neither admirers nor critics are likely to deny that the excellence of its greatest specimens reflects, and consciously reflects, the tone of a society whose rulers are divided by a chasm from the common herd. By the end of the first decade of the eighteenth century, native music is almost extinct; Handel, who first visited London in 1706, and Italian opera, rule alone. The domestic architecture of the well-to-do is sometimes distinguished, sometimes heavily pretentious; but whether majestic, or a mere monument of frigid ostentation, it bears its meaning on its face. Its aim is to be cosmopolitan, classical, less the enlargement of a native style than a repudiation of it. The drama, though not dead, is sick—sick of a resolute determination to be, before all things, genteel, with classical or foreign models to maintain an elevated tone, and smoking-room guffaws or drawing-room witticisms in place of humour. The prose is often admirable, but it also has changed; not imagination or eloquence, but lucidity, urbanity, decorum, are its characteristic virtues. The poetry is a well-managed instrument; at its best, a splendid exercise in the grand manner. Even the trifles tell the same story. As archaeologists know, there are worse clues to the convictions of a period than the tombs prepared by it for its dead. The characteristic feature of the sepulchral monuments of the Augustan age is not merely the chubby cherubim, too fat to fly, squatting heavily on some of them; it is the note struck in the epitaphs. Dreadful memories of fierce fanaticisms have caused 'moderation' to be the chief virtue selected for commendations; 'enthusiasm' has become the damning vice. The momentous discovery has been made that the words 'truly respectable' are a reliable passport to Heaven.

Whatever the crimes of the Elizabethans, respectability was not among them. From the Imperial Votaress, who was at home enough in the classics to chastise the indiscretions of a foreign ambassador in *ex tempore* Latin, but who also, when annoyed, swore in the vernacular like a fishwife, described the House of Commons as an assembly of devils, and boxed noble ears, to the drama, with the violence, buffoonery and hearty coarseness which have caused a foreign critic to denounce it as a riot of savages, and from the drama to everyday life, the note of it all was a genial, passionate vulgarity. The contempt, outside small circles, for the severer economic virtues—he 'lives like a hog' was a criticism passed, not on poverty-stricken squalor, but on the sordid parsimony of a noble miser—the emphasis on lavish expenditure, rather than income, as the mark of social status; the indiscriminate profusion of the great households; the readiness of peasants with a grievance to fly to arms; the horseplay of London apprentices mobbing an unpopular foreign dignitary with the cheerful indifference to the proprieties of a body of Chinese students, are all, in their different ways, examples of it. Nothing is common or unclean. Different sides of life are not kept in closed compartments, but fertilize each other. Eminent men are eminent in half a dozen different ways at once; among those who are not, work, amusement, religion, adventure and a little fighting, are all stirred in one bowl. Descriptions of Shakespeare as a lawyer, schoolmaster, soldier and sailor, as well as a poet and actor-manager, are not, it seems, according to light; but such versatility, had he shown it, would have been quite in the Elizabethan manner. Stubbe's *Anatomy of Abuses*, or half a century later, Prynne's appalling pamphlet in seven hundred folio pages, suggest that it was this intemperate catholicity, even more than graver lapses, which smelled to Puritans of Hell-fire, as it was Puritan fastidiousness, walking like a cat on ice, and talking sanctified commonplaces through its elevated nose, which made it hateful to the Sir Toby Belches, who had no objection to virtue in moderation, but liked cakes and ale as well. In the literature of the time there is plenty of all three. It takes its materials where it finds them, in Plutarch or Cheapside, in Gloucestershire or Montaigne; has friends at the cheerful address later invented by Bunyan, an Elizabethan converted and conscious of sin —'Flesh Lane, over against the Church, hard by *The Sign of the Conscience seared with a Hot Iron*'—reeks heavily of the soil, and is not ashamed of its origins.

That is so in the case of the art then most widely loved and practised. Miss Jones, in her admirable work on the Charity Schools of the eighteenth century, recounts that those of England, though not of Wales, excluded from their curricula singing and ballads—'profane and loose poems set to music'— as calculated both to corrupt the morals of the young, by encouraging them 'to put too great value upon themselves', and to undermine 'the grand law of subordination' on which society reposed.[1] Elizabethan authoritarianism had its seamy sides; but, if its hands were often rough, its nerves were good. Once firmly in the saddle, it was not frightened of its fellow-countrymen, and these refinements of precautionary zeal —today only too familiar—were foreign to its simple mind.

One of the first characteristics, indeed, of English life to strike observers was the diffusion among all classes of a passion for music. The styles of composers were not, it seems, unaffected by it. 'The new wave of musical activity in singing and playing in the second half of the sixteenth century,' writes a recent historian, 'proves most eloquently that the ordinary folk, especially the peasantry, were not only not incapable of creative thought, but a very important part of Elizabethan musical life. In turn, the art of the higher regions of society was most strongly influenced by the vigour in the cultural activities of the common people in their popular pageants, folk songs and dances. . . . The popular element was still prominently displayed in early Jacobean chamber music.'[2] It need not be assumed that works of individual genius—the madrigals and part-songs of Morley or the solo-songs of Danyell and Doweland—were consciously coloured, though they may have been, by folk-melodies. The significant fact is the existence of a public whose spontaneous appetite for musical enjoyment made it alert to welcome and transmit them.

Somewhat of the same might be said of the craft, whose range, next to agriculture, was the most extensive. The best so our local historians, Dr Hoskins of Leicester, has expressed the view that, in the eighty years between the accession of Elizabeth

---

[1] Mary Gwladys Jones, *The Charity School Movement: a Study of Eighteenth Century Puritanism in action* (Cambridge University Press, 1938).
[2] Ernest H. Meyer, *Elizabethan Chamber Music: the history of a great art from the Middle Ages to Purcell* (Lawrence & Wishart, 1946).

and the meeting of the Long Parliament, the greater part of rural England was rebuilt. The English climate is not kind to wooden buildings, and some of the finest seventeenth-century specimens of the art are to be seen, far from the country which created it, in the woodlands of New England; but there are regions, like the limestone belt, of durable structures where the truth of his statement is visible to the eye. Since, apart from occasional depressions, agriculture and textiles were doing well, everyone was building; and everyone had the same necessities to meet; the same rain to carry off; except for such natural differences as those which existed between the stone, wood and clay districts, the same materials to use; and, within those large divisions, much the same idea as to what a house should be like. Hence, apart from variations in size, which are, of course, striking, the style of most of the domestic buildings of the period—the smaller manor-houses and farms, the barns and cottages—tends, in a given locality, to be all of a piece. Like their owners, the two former have been up and down in the world a score of times. Only one who knows their individual histories can tell them apart.

In literature, since it is less directly a response to natural needs, the complexities are greater; but, here again, similar influences were at work. The proper starting-point, in considering them, is the character of common speech. When an Elizabethan spoke of 'my country', he commonly meant, not 'my nation', but what a Frenchman means by '*mon pays*'—my province, district or county. There are some grounds for thinking, though certainty is impossible, that most members of most classes, not excluding many of the gentry, talked dialect at home; but the terms employed are less significant than the attitude revealed in the manner of using them. Consider two quotations: 'As sheep or lambs are a prey to the wolf or lion, so are the poor men to the rich men'; 'Wicked people, in conditions more like to wolves or cormorants than to natural men, that do most covetously seek to hold up the late great prices to corn and all other victual by engrossing the same into their private hands . . . ; against which foul, corrupt fraud and malicious greediness there are both many good laws and sundry orders of late years given . . .' The vivid, concrete words, the anger expressed in a simple, hard-hitting phrase, are the same in both. But the first was a remark made by one of the Norfolk peasants who rose with Ket in the agrarian revolt that, seventy years later, was still recalled, as an awful warning, by speakers in the House during the debate on the first abortive general Enclosure Bill, and who was probably hanged in the course of the next fortnight; the second is part of an order on the subject of price-controls addressed by her Majesty's Privy Council to the Justices of Norfolk.[1] It is as though today a statement by the Ministry of Food were expressed with the violent directness of the language to be heard in queues, and the language of queues possessed the formal solemnity of Whitehall English, without its circumlocutions. That common quality of speech was not a mere trifle. Men spoke as they felt, and they felt as they lived. Since all, or nearly all, of them lived, as the Litany once a week reminded them, in intimate dependence on a capricious and tyrannical nature, their feelings on most subjects were much the same. Much is said and justly, of the ferocity of their religious conflicts. It is equally significant, though less often remembered, that those conflicts themselves could not have occurred but for the common premise supplied by a general agreement as to the transcendent importance of the ground of dispute.

Like all great literatures, that of Elizabethan England drank from many springs, foreign as well as native; but a community of understanding, which did not preclude sharp collisions of economic interest, was the soil in which it grew. Life, for all classes, was more spectacular, and, in a sense, more ceremonious, than it is today. Popular culture, before the Bible became a household book, was predominantly an oral and visual culture. Ballads, such as that which, when recited by a blind crowder, stirred the blood of Sidney; sermons; an occasional play; and social activities born of the daily intercourse of neighbours, were the food which fed it. The Bible itself, when added to them, offered incitements to almost too dramatic action. The imagination of common men worked at times with a

<hr />

[1] For the quotations, see *Original Papers of the Norfolk and Norwich Archaeological Society* (1905, p. 22), and *Stiffkey Papers* (Camden Society, Third Series, Vol. XXVI, 1915, p. 140); for the text of the enclosure bill of 1621, W. Notestein, F. H. Relf and H. Simpson, *Commons Debates, 1621*, Yale University Press, New Haven, 1935, 7 vols. Vol. VII, pp. 112–19; and for references by speakers to the revolt of 1549, *ibid.*, III, pp. 186–7, and V, pp. 148–9.

spontaneous intensity which an epoch that has starved it finds difficult to grasp.

The methods—one might almost say the ritual—of peasant risings, offer one example of its power. The mysterious leader —a Jack of the style, a Piers Plowman, a Captain Pouch 'sent of God to satisfie all degrees whatsoever', a Lady Skimmington —in the infancy of Elizabeth, the banner with a plough, and the four captains of Penrith, Faith, Pity, Poverty and Charity, who march with drawn swords round Burgh church; in the later years of her successor, the play composed by a village schoolmaster for the commoners of Kendal, in which landlords are shown as ravens tearing in hell the entrails of sheep, their tenants—such episodes reveal popular emotion creating naturally and swiftly, at moments of excitement, a symbolism to express it.[1] Some of the later proceedings, indeed, of the Diggers, who inherited that tradition, and whose name meets us in the Midlands half a century before Winstanley made it for a moment a word of fear, are best regarded, not merely as pedestrian essays in practical land reform, but as half-symbolical acts, bringing light to a people sitting in darkness by an ocular manifestation of the New Law of Righteousness.

The imaginative vivacity which, when fired by a crisis, produced the poetry of action, flowed, in the tranquil routine of normal life, through different channels, but was sustained and invigorated, not stifled, by it. In villages, a round of recurrent activities—May-games; Whitsun, Easter and Christmas festivities; Church-ales; yearly wakes; occasional 'gatherings for Robin Hood', such as, on one occasion, had deprived an indignant Latimer of his congregation; days off under Lords of Misrule, elected by 'all the wildheads of the parish', with followers in 'liveries of green, yellow or some light wanton colour; . . . about either leg twenty or forty bells', and 'hobby-horses, dragons and other antics'; now and then a performance

[1] For the first three leaders, see R. H. Tawney, *The Agrarian Problem in the Sixteenth Century* (Longmans, Green, 1912, pp. 318, 333-4); for Lady Skimmington, S. P. D., Chas. I, CXCIII, 66; CXCIV, 60, I-V; CCIII, 36; for the banner with a plough and four captains of Penrith, Tawney, *op. cit.*, pp. 318-19; for the play performed at Kendal in 1621, Mildred Campbell, *The English Yeomen under Elizabeth and the Early Stuarts* (Yale University Press, New Haven, 1942: Yale Historical Studies, Vol. XIV, pp. 150-3). Its occasion was a struggle over tenant-right in the barony of Kendal. The issue came before the Court of Star-Chamber, and was decided in favour of the tenants.

got up by Snug the joiner and Flute the bellows-mender, like that of which Shakespeare makes affectionate fun—in the larger villages called towns, gild pageants and plays, and sometimes, as at Gloucester, a 'mayor's play', which, as one who saw it as a child wrote long after, 'took such an impression on me that, when I came to man's estate, it was as fresh in my mind as if I had seen it newly acted'—these and similar diversions, if not universal, appear to have been widespread.[1]

Thus the taste for seeing life dramatized was not a novelty, but a long-established habit, which formed, like the seasonal tasks of the agricultural year, an inseparable part of the traditional stuff of everyday existence. The Elizabethan, like the Athenian, drama, was an eminently social thing. Such humble enjoyments added their mites to the miracles created by it. Its greatest period was short, and passed through several phases. In the first, from the 1580s to the early years of James, popular tastes appear to have predominated in the public theatre, and popular and courtly entertainments to have influenced each other. It is not surprising that the picture of Shakespeare's audience drawn by Mr Bennett, or, for that matter, by Ben Jonson—'capricious gallants', 'the rankest stinkard', 'the rude barbarous crew', 'a fellow that comes . . . once in five years, at a parliament time', interspersed with a majority 'very acceptive and apt to applaud any meritable work'—should remind us, in miniature, of the crowd at a cup-tie final.[2]

The Elizabethan spirit did not die with Elizabeth. The greatest of its literary achievements belong to the first half of

[1] For May festivities, church-ales, wakes and lords of misrule, see Philip Stubbes, *Anatomy of Abuses in England*, 1583 (Editor, F. J. Furnivall, New Shakespeare Society, 1877, pp. 146–54); for gatherings for Robin Hood, Hugh Latimer (Bishop of Worcester), *Sermon preached before Edward VI*, April 12, 1549, see *Seven Sermons preached before Edward VI* (Arber English Reprints, 1895), also *Sermons* (Everyman's Library: Dent); for the Mayor's play at Gloucester, R. Willis, *Mount Tabor: or Private Exercise of a Penitent Sinner*, 1639. As Willis was born in 1564, the morality play which so much impressed him *The Cradle of Security*, in which three ladies represented pride, covetousness and luxury; the prince, wickedness and two old men, the end of the world and the last judgement, was presumably performed at Gloucester some time in the 1570s. Useful selections from the above and other contemporary works will be found in *Life in Shakespeare's England* by J. Dover Wilson (Cambridge University Press, 1911; Penguin Books, 1944).

[2] H. S. Bennett, *Shakespeare's Audience*, Annual Shakespeare Lecture of the British Academy (Oxford University Press, 1944, see *Proc. Brit. Ac.*, Vol. XXX); Ben Jonson, *The Case is Altered*, Act II, Scene iv, see *Works* (Editors, C. H. Herford and Percy Simpson, *Oxford University Press*, Vol. III, 1927).

the next reign; and it survives, an intermittent voice, down to
and beyond the political breakdown. One hears the authentic
note in that charming poem, composed by—of all people—a
bishop,[1] 'Farewell Rewards and Fairies'. One encounters it in
another key, when, in turning over the business papers of a
City magnate on the road to high political office, one discovers,
scrawled by him on the back of a dull account,[2] the lines
ascribed to Raleigh on the night before his execution,

> E'en such is time, that takes on trust
> Our youth, our joys, our all we have,
> And pays us but with earth and dust. . . .

and realizes that there were moments when, for all his sanguine
self-assurance, the conqueror was visited amid his triumphs by
thoughts of the kind later immortalized in Shirley's justly
famous song. It meets us, in different guises, in that delightful
book, half biography, half the historical ramblings of the
humanest of antiquaries, John Smith's *Lives of the Berkeleys*;
or in Fuller's *Holy and Profane State* and *The Worthies of England*;
or in passages of Sir Thomas Browne; or later, a belated echo,
in Walton's *The Compleat Angler*, which, though not always
infallible—unless the capricious creatures have changed—
on the ways of trout, is admirable on human beings. But the
balanced society of the great age—economic interests encouraged, but kept in their place; authority masterful, but popular
sentiment a power—did not last. There were contemporaries
who realized, when the new century was still young, that
something had gone wrong.

[1] Richard Corbet, 1582–1634, Bishop of Oxford and Norwich, *A Proper New
Ballad intituled The Fairies Farewell or God-a-mercy Will*; 'to be sung or whistled to
the tune of the Meadow Brow by the learned; by the unlearned to the tune of
Fortune'. See *The Poems of Richard Corbet* (edited with biographical notes and a
life of the author by Octavious Gilchrist, Longmans 1807). This is the fourth
edition, with considerable additions. *The Fairies Farewell* is also reprinted in *A
Treasury of Seventeenth Century English Verse, 1616–1660* (Editor, H. J. Massingham,
Macmillan, 1919). Another edition is decorated by C. Lovat Fraser and privately
printed, London, 1916.

[2] *Cranfield MSS.* 6118. The account is contained in a letter to Cranfield from
one Richard Blackall, and gives particulars of customs duties received on Spanish
or sweet wines, in which Cranfield was financially interested. Blackall's letter is
dated from Exeter, October 18, 1618, and presumably reached Cranfield in the
course of the next week or ten days. Raleigh was executed on October 29, 1618.
Cranfield's version of Raleigh's lines differs slightly from that commonly printed
today.

The influence of the Court, the hypertrophy of the metro-
polis, the portentous inflation of the legal profession, the
supposed wickedness of Roman Catholics, the alleged hypocrisy
of Puritans, the advance of the money-power, were all put in
the dock. The favourite target of the dramatists was the last.
The greatest of all—

> Is not he just which all things doth behold
> From highest Heaven, and bears an equal eye?

—makes his own universe; but few, save he, are an exception
to the statement.

On the economic background of it all, I must not dwell. It
is sufficient to say that, with the Anglo-Spanish Treaty of 1604,
which wound up twenty years of conflict, followed two years
later by a Treaty of Commerce between England and France,
and later again by the twelve years' truce between Spain and
the Netherlands, Europe, though not without wars and
rumours of wars on her Eastern marches, slid half-unconsciously into one of her brief lucid intervals. The long commercial boom, which in England was one of the results of that
partial pacification, not only meant a sensational expansion of
international trade, but combined with the effects of continued
inflation and the opportunities offered by the financial necessities of the Government to produce a series of speculative orgies
on the London market, and a rash of new fortunes. Dekker,
whose charming picture of craft life in *The Shoemaker's Holiday*
is known to everyone, expresses the popular view of the
parvenu plutocracy and its values in the picture of the merchant,
Barterville, with his creed that

> Nature sent man into the world alone,
> Without all company, to serve but one,
> And that I'll do,

and the comment on that remorseless individualism passed
by his attendant devil: 'True City doctrine, Sir.'[1]

The verdict of a writer of loftier stature and far wider range
was not very different. There is, of course, much else in Ben

[1] Thomas Dekker, *If it be not good, the Devil's in it*, 1612, see *Dramatic Works* (Editor,
R. H. Shepherd, J. Pearson, 1873, 4 vols. Vol. III, p. 322).

Jonson; but, as Professor Knights[1] has suggested, some of his most admirable plays, with their company-promoters, land-grabbers and monopolists, are partly the criticism of a traditional code of social ethics on old vices on the way to be sanctified as new virtues. Middleton, who produced in *The Changeling* a play described by some as the greatest tragedy of the period outside Shakespeare, reveals in his comedies of London life a different aspect of the same transformation. Massinger's Sir Giles Over-reach, a satire on the notorious Mompesson, and his outrageous Lady Frugal, are studies, if diluted ones, on Jonsonian themes. All of these writers were too good artists to turn their plays into sermons. None of them, in observing the world about him, could fail to seize and express the erosion of accepted standards of social conduct, which was among its most conspicuous features.[2]

The situation which evoked such responses from the dramatists could be illustrated in a score of different ways, from rural lamentations at the supersession by sharp business men of the easy-going ways of the old-fashioned landlord, or the struggle of London craftsmen against capitalist encroachments, or the more general exasperation aroused by the multiplication of parasitic interests based on concessions wrung from royal favour, to the elaboration of the metropolitan money-market by the practitioners whom an economically half-sophisticated age denounced, while it courted them, as damnable usurers. It was accompanied by a second change, of equal significance. Dryden, in speaking of the vogue enjoyed at the Restoration by Beaumont and Fletcher, remarks of the latter that he 'understood and imitated the conversation of gentlemen much better' than Shakespeare.[3] In view of the volume and variety of their work, much of which, if it rarely

[1] L. C. Knights, *Drama and Society in the Age of Jonson* (Chatto & Windus, 1937). I should like to acknowledge my indebtedness to Professor Knights for ideas and illustrations.

[2] The following plays may, in particular, be mentioned in this connection: Ben Jonson, *Volpone, The Alchemist, The Devil is an Ass,* see *Works* (Editor, C. H. Herford and Percy Simpson, Oxford University Press, 1925–47, 8 vols. in progress, see Vols. I–VII); Thomas Middleton, *Michaelmas Term, The Roaring Girl, A Trick to catch the old one,* see *Plays* (Editor, A. H. Bullen, Nimmo, 1885–6, 8 vols.); Philip Massinger, *A New Way to pay Old Debts, The City Madam,* see *Best Plays* (Editor, A. Symons, Mermaid Series: Benn, 2 vols., 1904, etc.).

[3] John Dryden, *Essay of Dramatic Poetry,* 1668, quoted by Knights (*op. cit.,* pp. 294–6).

scales the heights, is pleasing, it would be less than just to say that they understood nothing else; but it is difficult not to feel, in reading them, that Dryden's praise has more than one edge. It is true that, by their time, the public for which plays are composed is ceasing to be the noisy, passionate crowd of the past, in which educated and illiterate, fastidious connoisseurs and lovers of horseplay and blood, had jostled each other. It is true that they are the dramatists, less of Shakespeare's hydra-headed multitude, than of polite society.

With them, and still more with Shirley and Brome, the later Comedy of Manners, which turns on the contrast between 'the good form' of the fashionable world and the 'bad form' of everyone outside it, is already on the way.[1] By, in fact, the accession of Charles, the days of comprehensiveness and profusion—the days of which it may be said, as Dryden said of Chaucer, 'Here is God's plenty', are drawing to a close. Interests formerly united fall apart. High spirits and a good conscience are less often than in the past at ease with each other. Imagination and reason begin to go their separate ways. Virtue becomes self-conscious. Poetry, some of it admirable, is more at home at court than in the tavern. The natural activities and amusements of men are a problem for moralists. Mercy and Truth, if they meet together, too often meet only to part. Righteousness is not deeply in love with Peace, and, in her austerer moments, strongly disapproves of kissing. Less than twenty years, and she is cutting Peace's throat.

The interplay between the practical activities of a society and the imponderables of emotion, moral sentiment and taste revealed in its art is not, of course, a feature peculiar to a single age. A reader who turns from the brief chapter in the life of a minute population—less than half that of greater London—to which this evening I have confined myself, to the two volumes of *Johnson's England*, edited by the late Professor A. S. Turberville, or to the works of Mr G. M. Young on its Victorian successor, will find on more crowded, and to many more attractive, canvases abundant illustrations of the same theme.

[1] J. L. Palmer, *The Comedy of Manners* (Bell, 1913, p. 91), puts the matter in a nutshell: 'there was form and there was bad form. The whole duty of man was to find the one and eschew the other'. For the work of Brome as an anticipation of later developments, see Kathleen M. Lynch, *The Social Mode of Restoration Comedy* (University of Michigan, New York, 1926, p. 34).

The significance of such affinities, it need hardly be said, is misconceived, when they are used as a basis for *naïvetés*, such as economic interpretations of culture. The day when these extravagances—half platitude, half fallacy—could be excused by the neglect of the factor emphasized by them is now long over. The oft-quoted words of Hamlet on the limitations of science, which he and his age meant by the word 'philosophy', and which continued to be so designated for another two centuries,[1] supply the proper comment on them.

The truth is that, apart from a few commonplaces, we know at present next to nothing of the relations, if such exist, between the artistic achievements of an epoch and the character of its economic life, and that the only candid course is to confess our ignorance. The attitude which best becomes us is a more modest one than the psycho-analytic ingenuity which discovers in great writers influences that they neither express nor would have understood. It is not to explain—whatever in such a connection that ambiguous word may mean—the efflorescence of genius. It is to rejoice in, admire and reverence its works. It is because the reading of History in conjunction with Literature may foster that attitude, that I have ventured to speak of them together.

[1] See, e.g., the titles of some university chairs of natural science. When Keats wrote à propos of the rainbow 'Philosophy will clip an angel's wings' and Wordsworth described a 'philosopher' as 'one who will peep and botanize upon his mother's grave', it was not to metaphysicians that the poets were referring.

POSTSCRIPT

AN APPRECIATION[1]

HUGH GAITSKELL

I have been asked to say a few words about Tawney. The surname alone seems abrupt. But it is what almost all of us called him.

I am most diffident about doing this. There are many others here who knew Tawney intimately and saw him more continuously than I. Moreover, he was a man of such stature that anything one says about him must seem inadequate.

I do not propose to talk about his career and achievements. I would, however, like to say something about his books—both the historical ones and the socialist ones. It seems to me that what gave them their special quality was the way in which they combined learning with passion. We all know scholars who are meticulous, thorough, hard-working and objective in their research and who yet fail to move their readers or give them any clear impression of the great tidal movements of history. We all know publicists who entertain and excite us, but about whose accuracy and objectivity we begin to have doubts.

But Tawney was both objective and moving. His writing reflected his own deep emotional convictions, yet he never allowed these to carry him away from the firm realities of serious historical research.

His two great socialist books—*The Acquisitive Society* and *Equality*—made a tremendous impact upon my generation —the generation which was born in the first decade of the century and grew to manhood in the 'twenties and early 'thirties. If you ask me why we were so impressed, I think it

[1] Address by the Rt. Hon. Hugh Gaitskell, c.b.e., m.p., leader of the Labour Party, at a Memorial Service for R. H. Tawney at St. Martin-in-the-Fields, on Thursday, February 8, 1962. One of the last acts in Hugh Gaitskell's life was to give his enthusiastic consent to the address being included in this volume.

was really for the same reason—that these books combined passion and learning. There was nothing false or exaggerated in them. In exposing the contrast between the Christian ethic and the actual condition of society, Tawney was drawing aside the veil and showing us what existed behind it. He was not inventing things, but simply showing them to us—things we had failed to appreciate before, but which we recognized immediately he wrote about them.

Of course, he was immensely helped by that most under-rated gift in public affairs—the capacity for writing beautiful English prose. Without this, he could never have communicated his thoughts and feelings as he did. I always think of him as *the* Democratic Socialist *par excellence*—an idealist who was rational-ist, a believer in liberty and equality—a man who loved his faith.

This morning, however, you will wish me to speak chiefly of Tawney as a man. We all have our memories of him. I remember our first meeting. It was in 1926, during the General Strike, when I was taken by Margaret Cole to see him in Mecklenburgh Square. There he was sitting surrounded by that appalling muddle of books, papers and used matches, which his friends knew so well, and wearing his sergeant's jacket from the First World War. It was the jacket which most impressed me. Somehow it was surprising that a member of the London School of Economics and the greatest socialist philo-sopher of his generation, should not only have a sergeant's jacket, but actually be wearing it. Somehow, too, it was heartwarming to see this.

It had its significance—not merely that he was not a pacifist, but that he was demonstrably and in one sense an ordinary person. There was nothing neurotic about him. I am not criticizing neurotics. Many geniuses have been neurotic; perhaps without the neurosis they would not have achieved what they did. But Tawney was just not like that. He was in no way neurotic. He was never blinded to reality by obsessions.

He lived an austere life, yet perhaps 'austere' is not quite the right word. It suggests something too harsh for Tawney. Certainly he was in no sense a puritan. He never sought to make other people live as he did. It was just the way of life he chose for himself.

Nor was there a trace of priggishness in his make-up. To mention the word in association with him is absurd. He lived by the clearest principles himself but he never sought to impose them on others.

Does this mean that he was tolerant? Tolerant he was of ordinary human frailties and weaknesses. But he was far too committed, too engaged, to be tolerant of everything. His intolerance, however, was concentrated on certain social relationships and the qualities associated with them. He hated servility and arrogance in any form.

As a speaker he never tried to create an effect yet, whenever he spoke, he could not help making a profound impression upon his audience. This was, I think, because he was utterly natural. He could never be histrionic or a poseur. He was just himself, and the personality that was himself was so remarkable that it made a deep impact on all who heard him.

He could be tough all right. Douglas Cole once told me he thought Tawney was the greatest man he knew. And when I asked why, he replied 'Because, apart from anything else, he could be ruthless'. Maybe the word is not quite appropriate, but his friends knew that Tawney was a very strong man.

Then there was his humility of which many have written. Possibly it is a dangerous word. He may not always have seemed so. He never hesitated to lay down the law to Ministers, or Universities or Governments. The point is rather that he never thought of himself in his heart as above or better than other people.

One of the last occasions on which I saw him illustrates this. We met in the house of some friends and talked about the Labour Party. He said he had been to his local Ward Party meeting where there had been some discussion about the constitutional relationship between the Annual Conference and the Parliamentary Labour Party. You will remember that not long ago there was some controversy on this. Tawney told me he thought the idea that the Conference would dictate policy to Members of Parliament was absurd. He said that no one had ever interpreted the constitution like this. 'But where,' he said, 'are the documents on all this? I feel I did not put the case sufficiently cogently. Can you help me to get some kind of brief, or is there a pamphlet setting it all out?' This was Tawney—at the age of eighty, 'The most distinguished economic historian of his generation,' by far the greatest force in adult education in the twentieth century, the leading socialist philosopher of our time—after attending his local labour party meeting.

Is all this too fulsome? Tawney would say that it was and probably be angry at such adulation. So let me mention some weaknesses. He was too uncompromising to be a very good worker in a team; he was at times impatient; he did not like small talk or social gatherings; he did not suffer all fools gladly all the time; he was abominably untidy and occasionally irritable; but when one has said that, one has just about scraped the barrel.

Looking back quite objectively, I think he was the best man I have ever known. The quality of his goodness was such that it never embarrassed you. You just accepted it as you accept genius.

There is a story about him and his friend Archbishop Temple. A friend said to Temple one day, 'What we need are more men like Tawney.' The Archbishop replied, 'There are no men like Tawney.'

We can only feel privileged to have known such a man and to have been his friends.